The Faithfulness of FAITH

C. E. COLTON

BROADMAN PRESS
Nashville, Tennessee

© Copyright 1985 • Broadman Press
All rights reserved
4215-34
ISBN: 0-8054-1534-3

Dewey Decimal Classification: 227.87
Subject Heading: BIBLE. N.T. HEBREWS // FAITH
Library of Congress Catalog Card Number: 85-9845

Printed in the United States of America

Library of Congress Cataloging in Publication Data

Colton, C. E. (Clarence Eugene), 1914-
 The faithfulness of faith.

 1. Bible. N.T. Hebrews XI-XII, 3—Meditations.
2. Faith—Meditations. I. Title.
BS2775.4.C6   1985   234'.2   85-9845
ISBN 0-8054-1534-3

Preface

The eleventh chapter of the Epistle to the Hebrews has been known through the years as "the roll call of faith." There is a rather lengthy list of persons who were renowned for their faith, people who stand out like great mountain peaks on the terrain of Old Testament history—Abel, Enoch, Abraham, Sarah, Isaac, Jacob, Joseph, Moses, Rahab, and other lesser knowns.

But it is more than just a roll call of faith; it is a kaleidoscopic review of faith, looking at it from many different points of view. Each view contributes something to our understanding and use of faith. I have sought in these meditations to point out the various features of faith as revealed in these human demonstrations. Here we are able to see something of the nature of faith, its effect upon life, and its application to the many different circumstances of life.

The first three verses of the twelfth chapter really belong to the eleventh chapter and can only be fully understood in the light of the eleventh chapter; therefore, I have included these verses in our series of meditations on faith. Then I have added a brief epilogue explaining the meaning of faith as related to salvation in the overall teaching of the New Testament.

Faith is a vital part of life, especially in the realm of religion. It is the means through which God bestows blessings, including the greatest blessing of all—eternal life. Therefore, we need to understand the basic meaning of faith and its place in our religion. While faith is indispensable for life and well-being both physically and spiritually, it must be kept in the background. Faith is like a pipe. We must have the pipe to bring the water to us, but, for the most part, the pipe lies hidden from view. It is the water which gives life, but we must have the pipe to bring that water to us. Some have elevated faith to a place of worship and have substituted it for God. This is a fatal mistake. Some have come close to this, if they have not actually done it. Some of the positive-thinking type of philosophy is at least perilously close.

We must have faith, for, as the writer of the Epistle to the Hebrews said, "without faith it is impossible to please [God]" (v. 6), but we must remember that God is to be exalted through faith and not our faith itself. When faith is kept in its proper place, it is a most vital factor in Christian living. These messages are designed to help the reader understand faith and to apply it in the proper place and in the proper manner. To this end I send this little book out with the prayer that it may accomplish that whereunto it has been sent.

C. E. Colton
Dallas, Texas

Contents

1
What Is Faith?

The eleventh chapter of Hebrews stands as one of the ten best-known and best-loved chapters of the Bible. It contains the great roll call of faith, including the outstanding people of the Old Testament. Inspiration is to be found in every verse of it, but it is best understood only as it is seen in the light of its relation to the chapters preceding and following it. This chapter is a part of that practical section of the epistle in which the author sought to inspire and challenge readers to greater fidelity in the service of the Christ.

After a clear and convincing presentation of the doctrine of atonement in Jesus Christ, the writer appealed to the readers in every conceivable way: first by direct exhortation, then by stern warning, and after that by a reminder of former fidelity. Then he sought to challenge them by pointing to the examples of people of faith, showing how their faith worked and with what reward. The testimonies of these people of faith must have been as convincing to the first readers as they are to us. If these people who lived during the period of lesser light exercised faith, how much more ought we to be strong in faith who have the fuller light of the New Testament revelation! We who believe can claim an identity with these great heroes of the faith. While they lived in the pre-Christian age, their faith was the same in essence as that which should characterize Christians of today. The tenth chapter closes with a statement which links our faith with that of these great people of the Old Testament: "But we are not of them who draw back unto perdition;

but of them that believe to the saving of the soul." With this
as the springboard, the writer proceeded to identify and describe these people of faith with whom we are to be identified.
But before relating the stories of faith bound up in these people,
he paused long enough to give a brief but impressive definition
of faith: "Now faith is the substance of things hoped for, the
evidence of things not seen" (v. 1).

Some people have insisted that this is not a definition of faith
but a simple statement about what faith does.[1] Realizing that
the very nature of faith makes it almost inexplicable, if this is
not a definition of faith, it is the nearest thing to it. It is a much
better definition than that which is found in Webster's dictio-
nary. I agree with A. C. Kendrick who said that "we thus have
a beautiful and complete definition of faith applicable to all the
causes to which the author proceeds to apply it."[2] That it is a
profound and significant statement on the subject no one can
deny.

As we attempt to analyze this picture of faith, we see three
aspects of the subject looming on the horizon: the sphere of
faith, the objectives of faith, and the effects of faith.

The Sphere of Faith

If we would understand what faith is, we must first understand in what sphere or realm it functions. Faith operates in
certain spheres; and outside of these spheres, it has no meaning
or use. Therefore, we need to understand the sphere of faith
which has been clearly identified in our text. Faith functions
in two areas: the future and the unseen. It has no place or
significance where we can see the answer to our questions.
Faith deals with that which is to be and that which is present
but unseen. These are identified in our text as "things hoped
for" and "things not seen."

To try to explain faith in the realm of the visible would be
like trying to explain a ship on a desert. For any adequate
understanding of faith, we must keep it within the bounds
assigned—the things to be and the things unseen. Some people

may seem to have little interest in these two areas of life. They are so completely absorbed in the present visible world of things that they have little time or incentive to think of the metaphysical or the future. In times of bereavement and distress, people's thoughts usually turn to the reality of the unseen. In the last analysis, the most cherished possessions of life are those which pertain to the realm of the unseen and the future.

The Objectives of Faith

We have noted the spheres in which faith functions. Now let us see just what faith does in these spheres. In things pertaining to the future, faith is "the substance." In things pertaining to the unseen, faith is "the evidence." A closer look at these words will shed more light on our subject.

The word *substance* which appears in the King James Version is a translation of the Greek word which means literally "to stand under." It refers to a foundation or that which gives assurance. Faith, then, is the ground on which one builds a hope. It very naturally glides into the idea of assurance or confidence. The American Standard Version uses the term *assurance.* Phillips renders it like this: "Now faith means that we have full confidence in the things we hope for."

Faith makes the future as sure as the present. It gives meaning and assurance to hope. Thus are hope and faith vitally and intrinsically related. Without faith, hope is nothing but the child of a wild and meaningless imagination. But faith gives foundation and meaning to hope, bringing it into the realm of that which is as sure as the present. Thomas Arnold remarked that faith "is that feeling or faculty within us by which the future becomes to our minds greater than the present."3 By faith the future becomes to us as real as the present.

In the realm of the unseen, faith gives "evidence" of reality. It is the idea of proof which the writer had in mind. Faith confirms the reality of things which cannot be seen with the physical eye. Because scientists deal so much with empirical evidence, some of them are tempted to categorize faith as unpardonable ignorance. They insist that there is nothing in the understanding which was not first perceived by some of the senses and that all the knowledge, which we naturally have, is originally derived from our senses. As explained by Leon Morris, "Faith extends beyond what we learn from our senses, and the author is saying that it has its reasons. Its tests are not those of the senses, which yield uncertainty."[4]

We are not at all surprised to find something like this coming from the minds of persons who have had no experience of faith. This would be the normal conclusion to be drawn where faith is not involved. One who has not experienced faith could never be expected to understand what faith is or what it does. In each of the senses there is a limitation to that which can be sensed. For instance, one could never be expected to know what seeing is like through the sense of hearing; nor can one know what hearing is like through the sense of seeing. One sense cannot ascertain what is being experienced by another sense. In like manner, one who has only the sense of physical touch could not be expected to understand what is understood by the sense of faith. One must experience faith in order to know what it is like; it can never be understood objectively apart from experience.

We may be able to see something of what faith does for others as we witness their actions, attitudes, and testimony. This may even be sufficient incentive to seek faith for ourselves, but until we come to experience faith for ourselves we cannot know what it means. One cannot describe or evaluate a sphere in which one has never entered. John Owen has expressed it like this:

> It is faith alone that takes believers out of this world whilst they are in it, that exalts them above it whilst they are under its rage; that enables them to live upon things future and invisible, given such a real subsistence unto their power in them, and victorious evidence of their reality and truth in themselves, as secures them from fainting under all opposition, temptation, and persecution whatever.[5]

The evidence which faith gives to the one who has faith is not necessarily an evidence or proof convincing to others. My faith may not prove anything to you; it will give proof to me of the reality of that which I cannot see. Marcus Dods gives this thought-provoking comment on our text:

> Substantially the words mean that faith gives to things future, which as yet are only hoped for, all the reality of actual present existence and irresistibly convinces us of the reality of things unseen and brings us into their presence. Things future and things unseen must become certainties to the mind if a balanced life is to be lived. Faith mediating between man and the supersensible is the essential link between himself and God.[6]

Just what are these unseen things which become real to men and women of faith? John Owen sums them up in this list: "God Himself, the holy properties of his nature, the person of Christ, and of the Holy Spirit, all spiritual, heavenly, and eternal things that are promised, and not yet actually enjoyed."[7] G. Campbell Morgan includes in his list things such as these: "God, the spirit world, the hidden forces; angels sweeping up the mountain side that the prophet saw and his servant did not see, the angel ministers watching Gethsemane, which Jesus saw and the disciples did not see."[8] Perhaps it would be impossible to give a detailed enumeration of all these "things unseen." Suffice it to say that faith brings into reality all that is untouched and unknown by the physical senses.

Nor can we say that all people of faith see the same unseen things. Some see more than others, and one may be able to see one aspect of the unseen world while another person may be able to see a different aspect. However, one thing is quite clear, namely, that through Christian faith all believers are enabled to see the reality of God in Christ as the one and only Redeemer. Through faith, men and women of the Old Testament were able to see the coming of a wonderful Messiah who would deliver the people from their sins. Through faith, we are able today to see this living Christ and to have fellowship with Him in a world which is unknown and unknowable to those who have no faith. It matters little whether one, through faith, is able to see fanciful sights in the metaphysical world or to communicate with loved ones in another world, but it is important to know that true Christian faith unveils the glory of the living and redeeming Christ. Any faith that does not make Christ real as the only Redeemer is not Christian faith. The first three verses of the twelfth chapter form the conclusion of this great discourse on faith. In these words, the writer appealed to his readers to look "unto Jesus the author and finisher of our faith" (v. 2).

The Effects of Faith

Faith has a tremendous effect upon the lives of those who experience it. This we shall see more clearly as we examine the life and conduct of the people whose lives are reviewed in this great roll call of faith. Taking a brief preview of the chapter, let us observe at this point some of the effects of faith upon the believer. What faith did for these men and women of old, it will also do for us. In looking over the chapter cursively, we see four outstanding characteristics of these men and women of faith.

First, they were obedient. Faith produces obedience. Where the unseen is not real, there is little incentive to obedience. But when by faith the unseen God is made real, obedience comes much easier. We are inclined to obey the God who is real, but who cares to obey a God who is not real?

Second, they were daringly courageous in the face of danger. Faith which brings reality to the unseen and assurance of that which is yet to be will produce a courage for faithful endurance in the face of the severest obstacles. Paul's faith in the assurance of the resurrection led him to face death daily and to jeopardize his life in the service of the Lord (1 Cor. 15:31). The same kind of faith will stir up courage in the fainting heart. We naturally withdraw from that which is unpleasant and difficult where there is no faith to make us sure of a possession over which the physical things of this life have no control. True faith is never completely without reason, but it is often daring beyond the point of human reason. Abraham, Moses, Elijah, and all the rest are demonstrations of this point. We must have a faith which takes us beyond that which we can see and feel with the physical senses. Only then will we ever have courage to face up to the trials and tribulations of this life.

Third, the faithful of the Old Testament had deep peace of mind. In spite of adverse circumstances, they seem to have had inner tranquillity which was outstanding. In choosing to endure afflictions with the people of God rather than to have the pleasures of Egypt for a season, Moses seems to have gained a sweet and peaceful soul repose. There is something about faith which stabilizes the soul even in the midst of the storm. Faith is the only thing that can stabilize the soul in times of deep distress. We cannot hope to have peace by maintaining peaceful physical circumstances. Nothing of the kind can be guaranteed in this world. History and experience have proved this. Our only hope for peace and tranquillity of soul is to be found in that sphere in which only faith can enter, a sphere in which the unseen becomes real and the future becomes as it were present.

Fourth, these faithful people inspired others. Indeed, that was the purpose in the mind of the writer in giving this review —to inspire greater faith on the part of his readers. The faith of one cannot prove the reality of the unseen to another, but it can inspire the other to seek the same experience of faith. The personal effects of faith are nonnegotiable; they cannot be transferred to another who has no faith. But the incentive to faith can be generated in one heart at the sight of faith in another heart. Many have been led to saving faith in Christ by observing the effects of faith in another. Let us so demonstrate our faith in Christ that others, seeing the fruit of our faith, may be inspired to embrace the same kind of faith and thus to experience for themselves these wonderful benefits of faith.

2
Faith and Creation

Having defined the sphere and nature of faith, the writer of the Epistle to the Hebrews proceeded to show how this faith expressed itself in people of the Old Testament. His first reference, however, was not to an individual but to a record. He showed how faith begins by the acceptance of the record of the beginnings of things as recorded in the Book of Genesis. "Through faith we understand that the worlds were framed by the word of God, so that things which are seen were not made of things which do appear" (11:3). This is a simple statement of faith concerning the Genesis account of creation. Although it is not a direct quotation from the Genesis account, it is an obvious allusion to it.

Thoughts on how things came to be have been occupying the human mind with varying degrees of interest since the beginning of recorded history. It is but natural that people should ask: "How did we get here?" "What is the original cause of the existence of human beings and the material universe in which we find ourselves?" Such questions have been clamoring for answers in the human mind. Many are still searching for an answer which will satisfy. To say the least, this subject is always of intense interest to thinking minds. I do not propose to answer all the questions pertaining to this subject in this brief discourse; nor could I do it if I had unlimited time and space. I would like to provide some thoughts on the subject and suggest some basic attitudes toward it as suggested in the words of our text. In doing so, I shall direct our thinking along these three lines: the mysteries of creation, some theories of creation, and the faith view of creation.

The Mysteries of Creation

Some aspects of creation will remain a mystery until we come into the fuller light of eternity. Persons of no mean ability have been studying this subject for ages, and, as yet, there is little more than theory or hypothesis. Volumes upon volumes of books have been written, and many theories have been proposed, but there is as yet no justification for a dogmatic proposition. At times, scientists have approached the dogmatic stage; but with the passing of time, other scientists have come along to contradict previous theories.

Out of all the investigation, research, and discussion on this subject one thing has been conclusively proven—the true facts concerning creation remain hidden from the human mind. It will likely continue to be an enigma. There are two areas in which science can never penetrate with success. One is the area of the distant past, and the other is the area of the distant future. Concerning the present, the immediate past, and the immediate future, science can probe and come out with fairly accurate and confirmed conclusions. But when science attempts to delve into the distant future, it degenerates into a system of speculation. Science is just as much at a loss when it seeks to delve into the distant past, back beyond the times of recorded history. Of course, archaeology and geology have made some contributions to this search into the distant past; but when we get back into the prehistoric ages, the evidence is not of such nature that any one can be scientifically dogmatic. We speak of scientific theories, but this is a misnomer. The very moment that science becomes theoretic it ceases to be science and becomes philosophy, offering theories and speculations instead of proven facts. Pure science must remain in the realm of proven facts.

There is nothing wrong in the search for more light on the distant past and the distant future, but we need to remember that much of the knowledge which we find in these two areas is in the form of speculative theory rather than proven fact. There is yet, no doubt, much more to be learned and much more that will be learned about the beginnings of our universe through the continued probing of scientific investigation, but when the last scientists have brought in their findings, there will still remain much that is unknown to the human scientific mind.

Some Theories of Creation

In the desire to find the answer to questions concerning the how and wherefore of creation, many interesting theories have been propounded. In the earlier days of philosophic investigation, the theories were simple though sometimes fantastic. One of these earlier theories was that the ultimate cause of all life was water since nothing seemed to exist without it. Another concluded that the ultimate cause was air; still another, change. Plato suggested that ideas were the ultimate cause of all life. Pagan religions have offered many different kinds of fanciful explanations of the beginnings of our world. Perhaps Socrates came closest to the Christian conception when he advocated the idea that somewhere there was an "overman" who was the ultimate cause.

In more recent centuries, theories have taken on a more scientific look even though they were still far from being scientific in the real sense of that word. Perhaps the most noted of all these theories is Darwin's theory, commonly known as evolution. Now there are almost as many variations of this theory as there are evolutionists. Basically, the Darwinian theory unfolds itself something like the following which has been taken from an article, by W. E. Denham, appearing in the *Southwestern Journal of Theology* for October 1921:

> Briefly stated, the theory is, that the universe as it now exists is the product of a gradual growth that has been going on for untold millenniums. In the long distant past, how long is widely

disputed, there was a time when nothing existed except a single life cell. Where this cell came from, how it had existed through the millenniums that had preceded, whether it had an eternal existence or had sprung spontaneously into being, we are not told. The theory goes no further than the existence of the cell. At some time in eternity this cell became subject to the influence of a force. The same questions relative to this force remain unanswered as to the cell. As a result, however, of the meeting of force and cell, development began, and from that single cell, through the millenniums that it must have taken, there has come the development of all the various forms of animate and inanimate matter. According to this theory we are still developing. Man is simply a higher form of the ape, the ape a higher form of some other animal, and so on until the lowest form of life is reached, then down through inanimate matter.[1]

This is the basic idea, but in recent years the theory has gone through many revisions. One of the latest versions is that which is known as theistic evolution. The theistic evolutionist accepts the basic idea of evolution as described above but adds the idea that God or some Supreme Being is responsible for that little cell.

Harold B. Kuhn, in an article which appeared in *Christianity Today*,[2] summed up the modern-day, non-Christian theories of creation under four heads: (1) Some regard the universe as being the result of self-origination; (2) others imagine it to be some sort of unfolding or emanation of a divine being; (3) still others believe that some form of eternally existing chaos has been posited which an intermediate "creator" fashioned into a cosmos; (4) others look upon the visible universe as an illusion. Time and space do not permit a detailed delineation of these theories. This brief summary will serve to show the variety of thought in trying to explain our material universe.

The Faith View of Creation

Over against all of these rather complicated and yet unconfirmed theories of creation stands the simple account which has been recorded for us in the first book of our Bible. This account of creation has no more scientific basis than any of the others. If evaluated on the basis of scientific proof, it would have to be eliminated along with all of the others. On the other hand, it does have as much scientific basis as any of the others. The fact is that no theory exists which can be *scientifically* proved. Any theory must be accepted, at least in part, by faith or not accepted at all.

In discussing the difference between a "chance" or a "choice" view of creation, W. B. Tolar explains that

> both "chance" and "choice" explanations are actually "faith" statements. It is not knowledge versus faith; it is faith versus faith. Man was not there. He does not actually "know;" he really only believes—regardless of his explanation. One may believe it happened this way or that (and have "evidence" for his belief), but it is still a faith explanation. The person who believes in God and believes that God created the world, believes in "choice" and should openly admit that his is a faith statement. But a person who believes it began by sheer chance or who does not believe God created the world is exercising an amazing faith also and should openly admit that his is a faith statement. Thus a person can believe in chance or choice.[3]

It is interesting to note that the Texas School Textbook Committee passed a ruling in 1984 that all science textbooks used in Texas public schools must identify all views of creation as theories only, whether creationist or otherwise.

Christian faith contains within it the desire to accept as true the biblical account of all things. Christian faith is faith in Christ. But where do we learn of this Christ? Is it not in the Word of God which we call the Bible? We first believe the account of Christ as revealed in the Word, then we believe in Him personally by faith. Is it not reasonable to suppose that those who have found the Bible to be true in its claims concerning the Christ will also be inclined to accept the accounts of the Bible on other matters?

We accept the biblical account of creation, not because we

understand it all or because it has been scientifically proved, but by faith. If I must accept any theory by faith, why not accept the theory which has been offered in the Book which has revealed to me the truth concerning Christ, my Redeemer? This is the very conclusion which was drawn by the author of Hebrews in the words of our text. There are many details which we do not understand, but we do understand by faith that "the worlds were framed by the word of God, so that things which are seen were not made of things which do appear" (11:3). From this statement, which we also accept by faith, we may draw three conclusions:

First, we understand that the material universe did not spring forth out of material substance, whether of itself or of something outside of itself. With this understanding, we at once exclude the Darwinian theory of evolution. Such an ordered universe as this with its minute and amazing laws of operation simply could not come into existence out of some impersonal material object. Sheer reasoning alone would not allow such a theory as this. Quoting again from W. B. Tolar, "Is it so gullible, so naive, so credulous to choose the faith answer called 'choice'? Does it really take more faith? Is it really more gullible than the other faith answer called 'chance'?"⁴ By faith we agree with the writer of the Hebrew Epistle that "things which are seen were not made of things which do appear."

Second, we understand that the unseen source of creation was a personal God. This is the positive side of the picture. It is the only alternative if we accept the foregoing conclusion that things material did not come from things which are seen. There is only one other way to account for them, namely, that a personal God brought them into existence out of nothing. They were framed "by the word of God." In this phrase, there is the hint that the universe was not only created by God but also came into being by the fiat of God. It is not the familiar term *logos* which appears here but the term *hrēma* which carries the idea of the spoken word or direct command. It is not enough to believe that God created the universe through some impersonal and indirect process over a period of ages. True Christian faith is that which accepts the idea of the creation of this universe by direct fiat of God. This is the biblical view, and the true Christian will be inclined to accept this view by faith.

Third, we understand that this same personal God who brought the universe into being by direct command also coordinates its various parts and now holds them together in keeping with His eternal purpose for it. This idea is implied in the verb, along with the substantive which is associated with it, which we find in our text. The verb is *katartizō,* which means to "fit together or make complete." The substantive appears in the King James Version as "worlds." Perhaps a better rendering would be "ages." The idea thus expressed is this: God not only brought the material universe into existence but also gave to it shape, order, and consistent form. It also suggests that there is more to creation than materialistic form; it involves the "ages," that is, time and history. God not only created and controls the physical universe in which we live but also guides and controls the destiny of this world with the human beings whom He has placed on it. God does have "the whole wide world in His hands."

Faith which accepts the fact of divine creation as recorded in the Genesis account is necessary and expedient, but we must remember that it is only the beginning of faith. Faith, as we shall see in the unfolding review of history as recorded in the eleventh chapter of Hebrews, *begins* with a recognition of the universe as a direct creation of God, but it is not finished until it follows the arrows of God's progressive revelation to the Christ of the cross and of glory. We do not know all of the details of God's purpose for His created universe, but we do know that this purpose is to be fulfilled and consummated in Jesus Christ, His Son. Happy are those who receive Him by faith and serve Him by faith.

3
Faith's Perception

"By faith Abel offered unto God a more excellent sacrifice than Cain, by which he obtained witness that he was righteous, God testifying of his gifts: and by it he being dead yet speaketh" (11:4). With this statement the writer of Hebrews began a series of references to outstanding Old Testament people as examples of the meaning and significance of faith. In this statement, we also have another occurrence of the use of that comparative adjective *better;* however, in this instance it is translated "more excellent." It is not the same word as that which is translated "better" in 10:34 and in a number of other places in the epistle. This same word does appear in 3:3. The word which appears in our text is often used to express comparison in quantity (the idea of more), but it is also used as an expression of quality, as in Matthew 12:41: "a greater than Jonas is here." We must conclude, therefore, that the word as used in our text carries essentially the same meaning as the other word which appears more frequently in the epistle. Abel offered up unto God a *better* sacrifice.

A cursory reading of the text will most likely leave the reader a little astounded and perplexed. On the surface, it does not seem fair to say that Abel's sacrifice was better than Cain's. But a more careful exegesis of the verse in the light of the Genesis account will bring out the deeper meaning and significance of this better sacrifice. Several aspects of the subject cry out for attention, such as: the cause of Abel's better sacrifice, the nature of Abel's better sacrifice, the attitude behind Abel's better sacrifice, and the results of Abel's better sacrifice.

The Cause of Abel's Better Sacrifice

We must not overlook the prepositional phrase with which this fourth verse begins: "By faith." In all of these examples taken from Old Testament history, the writer sought to show that faith lies behind all right actions toward God. Whatever Abel did which was pleasing to the Lord, he did it because faith prompted and inspired it. Grammatically speaking, there are two possible ways to relate this prepositional phrase to the sacrifice itself. Marcus Dods raised this pertinent question: "Does the writer mean that faith prompted Abel to make a richer sacrifice, or that it was richer because offered in faith?"[1] The former alternative is the one which has been followed by most interpreters and seems to be most suitable to the context. There certainly was an element of faith involved in the sacrifice which was pleasing to God, but the writer of Hebrews seems to be saying that such a better sacrifice grew out of an attitude of faith.

In all religious exercises, faith is prerequisite. Faith prompts the exercise and also gives insight into its deeper meaning. Whatever one does which is acceptable to God has faith as its basis and inspiration. Without faith, one cannot begin to serve God acceptably. This is the premise upon which all genuine religious action is based. Experience with God is born out of faith and is nurtured by faith.

The Nature of Abel's Better Sacrifice

We learn from the Genesis account that Abel's better sacrifice consisted of "the firstlings of his flock and of the fat thereof" (4:4). Abel was a keeper of sheep, and he took the very best specimen to be found in his flock and offered it up as a sacrifice to God. The lamb was slain and then placed upon an altar to be burned.

The inferior sacrifice of Cain consisted of "the fruit of the ground" (v. 3). It was but natural that Cain should bring something from the fruit of the ground since he was a tiller of the soil. It was also natural that Abel should bring something from the flock since he was a keeper of sheep. We must go behind the sacrifices themselves to find the secret of Abel's better sacrifice. Surely the difference could not have been in the substance of which the sacrifice consisted, for both men brought of the fruit of that work in which they were engaged. The substance, we must say, does have a significance in pointing to something deeper, but in and of itself there can be no distinction in quality. Both gifts came out of that which God had created. For the true significance of the superior sacrifice of Abel, we must go beyond the mere nature of the offering.

The Attitude Behind Abel's Better Sacrifice

The sacrifice itself does suggest something concerning the attitude of the worshiper, and the account in Genesis confirms these suggestions. There is no reasonable justification for the difference between the two sacrifices unless it is to be found in the attitudes of the two men who offered up the sacrifices. What was the difference in the attitudes of the two men? It should be noted that first the Lord had respect "unto Abel" and then "to his offering." "But unto Cain and to his offering he had not respect" (Gen. 4:4-5). It was an acceptance and rejection of the person first and then the person's offering. This indicates that the secret of the better offering lay in the man rather than in the offering, but the offering itself reflects something of the attitude of the man.

There are differences of opinion, however, among Bible scholars as to the exact identity of this attitude. Some, like Philip Edgumbe Hughes, insist that the attitude refers to the word *faith* at the beginning of the verse. Hughes explained that "faith is the ruling concept of this verse, and indeed of the whole chapter, as the emphatic position of faith at the beginning of the sentence attests, and accordingly faith not sacrifice is the proper antecedent of the relative pronoun, which."[2] Others, like B. F. Westcott, prefer to take Abel's sacrifice, rather than his faith, as the antecedent of the relative pronoun. Westcott explained that "the sacrifice was the sign of righteousness —the true relation to God by faith—which he had inwardly."[3] Looking at it from the standpoint of the sacrifice, in what way or ways were these two men different in their attitudes toward themselves and toward God? There is no good reason, as some have done, to charge Cain with insincerity. We cannot believe that the difference lay in the fact that Abel was sincere in bringing his offering and that Cain was insincere. Both men appear to have been equally sincere in their desires to offer up sacrifices to God. There is nothing to indicate that Cain had an ulterior motive in bringing the offering to God.

The secret then, in being acceptable to God, does not lie in sincerity alone. Many have been led to believe that as long as a person is sincere in whatever he does, especially in religious exercises, he is acceptable to God. But this is one of the most disastrous errors ever perpetrated on humanity and has its source in the devil himself. Many have been lulled into a state of false peace and complacency by this heresy. It is one of the most popular philosophies of our day. It is sheltered under the roof of such seemingly altruistic virtues as toleration, broadmindedness, freedom, and universalism. The proponents of such a philosophy would have us to believe that there is one virtue only by which we find acceptance before God and that virtue is sincerity.

I would not want to cast any unfavorable reflection upon the virtue of sincerity. It is a virtue of highest order. Certainly God is never pleased with insincerity, but the point I emphasize here is that sincerity alone is not enough. There must be sincerity, of course, but there must be more than sincerity. Two persons may be equally sincere. One will go to heaven at death and the other to hell; one will be acceptable before God, and the other will be rejected. The experiences of Cain and Abel constitute a case in point. If we are to discover the secret of Abel's better sacrifice, we must go deeper than the idea of sincerity.

Two vital factors in our relation to God are implied in the story of Cain and Abel. These two factors are not clearly stated as they are in the fuller light of New Testament revelation, nor should we expect them to be. We must remember that Cain and Abel lived in the very dawn of human history. The idea of redemption had just been introduced to the human mind. One should not expect to find here a comprehension of redemptive truth equal to that which was experienced by the apostle Paul following the appearance of the Christ on earth. It was not that Abel had a different conception of truth than did Paul; it was only that Abel saw but hazily what the apostle saw in its fuller and clearer expression. The essential or basic truth was the same; but in the day of the dawn of human history, Abel was able to see but dimly. What he did see was basic truth, and it was sufficient to place him in an acceptable position before God.

The first of these two basic factors which were comprehended, even if but dimly, by this second son of our first parents was that of a consciousness of sin. The sacrifice of the lamb, which was the offering up of one living thing for another, a substitution, suggested that in Abel's mind there was the consciousness of unworthiness in relation to God. This thought is brought into clearer light by the apparent opposite attitude of Cain. Cain seems to have brought the fruit of the ground with an attitude of pride, showing God what he had done. It was the idea of showing off before God rather than an humble confession of sin. The reflection of this attitude on the part of Cain is best seen in the turn of events which followed the offering up of the sacrifices. If Cain's had not been an attitude of pride, he probably would not have become so bitter and resentful of his brother when Abel's sacrifice was accepted. The ugly conduct of Cain seems to prove the presence of an unwholesome attitude before the offering was made.

Humility leads to love and respect, but an attitude of pride issues in feelings of resentment, bitterness, and querulous criticism. Resentment and bitterness toward others do not constitute the causes of God's rejection; they are simply the results of an attitude of pride. God always rejects pride in people. "For God resisteth the proud, and giveth grace to the humble" (1 Pet. 5:5). We do not gain God's favor by exhibiting our good qualities before Him. He wants a broken and contrite heart. Cain came with head high to impress God with his accomplishments, but Abel came with head low to acknowledge his sinfulness.

Herein is the first principle in the experience of salvation. All who believe in a salvation by works, like Cain, seek to gain God's favor by what they themselves have accomplished. Such expressions of false pride, and they are all false, are repulsive to God. When such people are told of their rejection by God, they usually, like Cain, begin to resent, criticize, or injure those who have been accepted of God through a sincere confession of sin. "Pride goeth before destruction" (Prov. 16:18).

The other factor which is involved in a successful approach to God is the consciousness and acceptance of a substitute redeemer. Recognizing the fact of sin only shows up our predicament; but we are never ready for the solution until first we realize our predicament. For that reason, one who recognizes his sinful state before God is only a short step from entrance into God's presence. For when once we see our great dilemma, God immediately reveals the Lamb who has already offered up Himself as our sacrifice for sin. It would be foolish to suggest that Abel had a clear understanding of the coming of Jesus Christ to earth and of Christ's atonement on the cross. Of course, Abel knew nothing of the details of such a plan, but perhaps he did sense the need for an atonement for his sins by the sacrifice of something innocent. Abel did have a hazy perception of the idea of atonement. That attitude and understanding made him and his offering acceptable unto God.

It is not enough to recognize our sinful condition. This, to be sure, must come first and is a prerequisite to the second, but our acceptance before God is not complete until we come in the consciousness of our sins to accept the blood of Christ as atonement for sins.

The Result of His Better Sacrifice

This better sacrifice brought God's approval and smile upon Abel. We are not told in what manner God indicated approval of Abel's offering. A tradition claims that approval was indicated by a fire which swept down out of heaven and consummed the sacrifice on the altar, as in the case of Elijah's sacrifice on Mount Carmel. This might have been true, but there is no record of it in the scriptural account. Probably there was some kind of a visible indication to Cain and Abel of God's response to their sacrifices.

God still gives indication of His approval of our sacrifices to Him, but usually these are not given in visible form. An inner voice speaks to our souls, telling us that we have been accepted of the Beloved. Simple assurance comes through faith when we know that we have followed the scriptural plan in our attempt to approach a holy God. By faith, the evidence is made clear of our acceptance before God.

There is still another result growing out of this better sacrifice. Through this better sacrifice, Abel was able to perform a continuing ministry. Even though he was soon killed by his jealous brother, he still speaks. "He being dead yet speaketh" (v. 4). Some commentators maintain that this speaking has reference to the speaking of Abel's blood which cried out from the ground against the injustice which was committed by this first murderer in human history, and thus it is a continuing voice against the sin of murder (Aquinas, Grotius, Owen, Delitzsch, Alford, and F. F. Bruce). There may be an element of truth in this; and, to be sure, the experience of Cain and Abel does speak against the evil of murder.

But Abel speaks to us in another way. He speaks to us of the fact of sin and the necessity of atonement. The better sacrifice of Abel points to the better sacrifice of Christ on Calvary. Abel's sacrifice was better than the sacrifice of Cain, but the sacrifice of Jesus was better than the sacrifice of Abel. The writer of the Epistle to the Hebrews brought out this thought very forcefully in the twelfth chapter: "To Jesus the mediator of the new covenant, and to the blood of sprinkling, that speaketh better things than that of Abel" (12:24). Abel's sacrifice was better because it points us to the better sacrifice of Jesus on the cross, through which every person must come in order to be accepted before God.

4
Faith and Fellowship

The second name in the rather long list of the heroes of faith is that of Enoch. Here we have a brief commentary on the Genesis account (5:21-24):

> By faith Enoch was translated that he should not see death; and was not found, because God had translated him: for before his translation he had this testimony, that he pleased God. But without faith it is impossible to please him; for he that cometh to God must believe that he is, and that he is a rewarder of them that diligently seek him (11:5-6).

We know very little about Enoch. Enoch's name appears only five times in the sacred Scriptures: twice as a name in a genealogical table (1 Chron. 1:3 and Luke 3:37), once in the Epistle of Jude (v. 14), and the other two times as indicated above. However, his name comes up frequently in the apocryphal writings. The reference in our text is little more than a repetition of the story as told in the Genesis account; and in that instance, it is only a part of a genealogical list. However, Enoch was more than just a name. The author of the Pentateuch took time from his genealogical listing to characterize Enoch. It is a most refreshing diversion from the long and somewhat monotonous list of names. One may almost go to sleep reading over this long list of men who lived, begat children, and died. But suddenly the reader is aroused by a juicy bit of diversion which breaks the monotony. It is like an oasis in the desert. Marcus Dods observed that "in the dry catalogue of antediluvian longevities a gem of faith is detected."[1] The others simply lived and died, but Enoch was different. He was a righteous man in an evil generation. He was about the only bright spot in a bedarkened civilization.

Even though we know very little about Enoch, what we do know about him is enough to convince us that he deserves a place in the roll call of faith. No higher compliment could be paid a person than to say that he "walked with God" (Gen. 5:22) or that he "pleased God" (v. 5). That tribute was paid to Enoch by the men who were inspired to write the Holy Scriptures. A serious study of this unusual man of faith can be most rewarding. We approach our study, therefore, with anxious anticipation. Since the emphasis of this eleventh chapter of Hebrews is upon faith, we should consider each person named in the light of his or her faith. Let us, then, consider the faith of Enoch in three respects: its content, its immediate issue, and its ultimate reward.

The Content of Enoch's Faith

In the insertion (v. 6) which serves to show the continuity of the chapter with regard to faith, the writer of the epistle summarized the content of Enoch's faith. He had in mind the faith of Enoch when he said, "He that cometh to God must believe that he is, and that he is a rewarder of them that diligently seek him." According to this explanation, faith must include two things: a belief that God exists and a belief that God is a rewarder of those who seek Him. Here we have the two elements which were suggested in the definition of faith as given in the first verse of the chapter. To believe that God exists is to make the unseen real; to believe that He will reward those who seek Him is to give assurance to that which is future. Thus do we have the "substance of things hoped for, the evidence of things not seen." But let us take a little closer look at these two elements in the content of faith.

One must begin by believing that God exists. This involves, of course, that which is unseen, for God cannot be seen with the physical eye. He is Spirit. But the assuming of such faith should not be too difficult, for persons are born with an innate proclivity toward belief in a divine being. It is natural and normal for persons to believe in a divine being or divine sovereignty. Dr. G. Campbell Morgan is right in contending that "effort is required to disbelieve rather than to believe."[2] Belief in the existence of God is a most natural activity of the human soul. Concerning belief in the existence of God, the child does not go from disbelief to belief; rather, the child goes from belief to stronger belief or to unbelief. A person's first impression is to believe.

Another factor which makes belief in God's existence rather easy is the evidence implied in the marvels of God's creation. One cannot study the marvels of nature and human nature without concluding that there must be one great divine Creator behind it all. Such marvels as we see in nature could not just happen to fall accidentally into existence. They must be the handiwork of a wise and sovereign God. In discussing the issues which we must face, Dr. W. A. Criswell gave this interesting analogy:

> We might as well believe that one could throw up letters of the alphabet and have them come down in the form of an Aristotelian treatise on Greek drama as to believe that blind, inert matter could ever create human soul and human personality.[3]

We who are Christians have the additional evidence of divine revelation and experience. To those who are spiritually blind, there is no value in the testimony of Scripture or the testimony of other Christians. To quote again from Dr. Criswell, "To the spiritually blind, God does not exist. To the spiritually deaf, God does not speak. To the spiritually dead, God does not live."[4]

Faith must begin with belief in the existence of God, but that is not enough to satisfy the requirements of the Divine Being. Faith which ends with a mere belief in the existence of God is not adequate faith. One must also believe that God will reward those who diligently seek Him. This does mean, as some have suggested,[5] that one must believe in the moral government of God, that God is moral in nature, and that His dealings with men are upon a moral plane. But it means more than this.

The phrase "of them that diligently seek him" should not be overlooked in any consideration of the meaning of this verse. The reward is promised not to those who seek that which God has or that which He is able to give but to those who seek *Him*. Many people seek what God has, but few seek *Him*. By faith, I know that God exists; by that same faith, I know that He can be found and known. With such faith, I go out in search of God. He can and will be found by those who search for Him with this kind of faith. The reward is in finding Him. When one goes out in search of God through genuine faith, one will find God. Such faith will lead one through the pages of the sacred Scriptures to Jesus Christ who is the Way, the Truth, and the Life.

The Immediate Issue of Enoch's Faith

We have seen that true faith is a belief that God exists and "that he is a rewarder of them that diligently seek him" (v. 6). The immediate result can be seen in the example of Enoch. So far as Enoch was concerned, the issue of faith was the pleasure of God and fellowship with God.

First of all, faith pleases God. God is pleased when His creatures turn toward Him in simple faith seeking His presence. He is not particularly pleased with those who come to Him once in a while in order to get something which they think God is able to give. But He is highly pleased when people seek Him just because they want to know Him.

The immediate effect of God's pleasure is the opening of the door into His presence. The greatest reward of faith is fellowship with God, and those who really seek Him will find Him. This, of course, was the purpose of God in creating people—that He might have fellowship with those who are created in His image. People were created for fellowship with God. They are the only form of creation which is capable of fellowship with God. A cow could never have a sense of fellowship with God;

there is no possible means of communication. Only people have a capacity for communion with God. Such communion was enjoyed in the early days of human experience in the garden of Eden. God and humans walked together, but then came disobedience and sin, and the fellowship was broken off. When sin came, that beautiful, intimate fellowship with holy God was broken. There was a separation between humanity and God.

This separation was a sad one, but God, in His infinite wisdom and love, provided a way by which this breach could be healed. People could not make the correction in their own strength, for sin had left them helpless and doomed. The reconciliation had to be initiated by God. This He did by sending His own sinless Son to be the propitiation for our sins. Thus, in Christ the breach was healed, and we may return to fellowship with God.

But sadder still was the fact that most people did not avail themselves of this remedy. Therefore, they remained outside the circle of fellowship with the Divine. Now and then faith would triumph, and a person would look to the coming of this Redeemer in order to find restoration of fellowship with God. This is what Enoch did. His faith was rewarded by fellowship with God. He and God became bosom friends; they walked together down the road of life; they communed with one another and enjoyed the blessedness of a sweet fellowship. Such fellowship with God is in reach of every person, and more so now than in the days of Enoch, for we who live on this side of the coming of Christ have the fuller light of New Testament revelation. If Enoch, in the dark days of the early dawn of civilization, could find fellowship with God through faith, how much more ought we to find blessed fellowship with God through Christ Jesus, our Lord!

The Ultimate Reward of Enoch's Faith

The immediate issue of faith is fellowship and acceptance with God, but this is not all of it. Much of the reward is still future. Faith sees reality in the unseen present, but it also looks

into the unknown future to find assurance of better things yet
to be. The testimony of Enoch's life tells us two things. First,
through faith we overcome death. "Enoch was translated that
he should not see death; and was not found, because God had
translated him" (v. 5). The word *translate* means "to be transferred from one place to another." There is a sense in which
every Christian is translated at death, but for Enoch this seems
to have been an instance of missing death altogether. It appears that Enoch did not go through the experience of dying as
other people do. It would seem to indicate that the body of
Enoch disappeared. Only one other person in all history is
known to have been transferred from earth to heaven without
dying. That person was Elijah, who was taken up in a chariot
of fire. Skeptics who are prone to doubt the credulity of all
miracles will reject the idea that these two men did not die, but
the fact remains that no one has yet been able to come up with
any undeniable scientific proof that it did not happen. Until
such proof is in hand, I will keep on believing the record as
given in the Bible.

We are not to conclude from this that anyone who has sufficient amount of faith can expect to be translated without dying
as was Enoch. God has given to us no promise of any such thing.
These two cases were exceptions to the rule and were allowed
to accomplish a divine purpose. Philip Edgcombe Hughes has
suggested that "Enoch, indeed, may be seen as a sort of proto-
type (together with Elijah at a later period) of the men and
women of faith who will be living at the moment of Christ's
return—an occasion of surpassing glory—and who, too, will be
caught up to be with Christ without passing through the experience of death."[6] We may conclude, however, from this experience of Enoch that all who, by faith in Christ, walk with God
will ultimately overcome death by being translated into a better world. The ultimate reward of faith, then, whether for
Enoch or for us, is the overcoming of death. We may not be able
to avoid the experience of death as did Enoch, but we can avoid

the fear and power of death to destroy. Through faith we come down to death's door only to be transported through it into something better.

That something better is a sweeter and more intimate fellowship with God. Whatever heaven is like, one thing is sure—it means that we will be privileged to have fellowship with God in a sweeter and more intimate relationship than was possible on earth. This is the ultimate reward of Christian faith. We learn to walk with God by faith on earth in order that we may be able to walk with Him more intimately in heaven. Someone has suggested that Enoch walked with God so long and so far that when he came toward the close of his earthly journey, God said to him, "Enoch, it's closer now to My heavenly home than it is back to your earthly one, so just come on up now without having to go back through the earthly valley of death." This may be fanciful thinking, but there is an element of truth in it. Heaven is just a closer walk with God. It is the ultimate goal toward which all believers look. If we would walk with Him in that "land beyond the river," we must learn to walk with Him here and now by faith; let us all remember that if we would walk with God, we must go God's way. Faith does not say, "Lord, come and walk with me," but "Lord, show me Your way, and let me walk with You in it until we can walk together in the sweeter fellowship of heaven." I. B. Sergei has expressed this thought in the following beautiful poetic words:

> My God and I, go in the field together,
>   We walk and talk as good friends should and do,
> We clasp our hands, our voices ring with laughter,
>   My God and I, walk through the meadow's hue.
>
> He tells me of the years that went before me,
>   When heav'nly plans were made for me to be,
> When all was but a dream of dim conception,
>   To come to life, earth's verdant glory see.

My God and I, will go for aye together,
We'll walk and talk and jest as good friends do.
This earth will pass and with it common trifles,
But God and I, will go unendingly.[7]

5
The Tokens of Faith

"By faith Noah, being warned of God of things not seen as yet, moved with fear, prepared an ark to the saving of his house; by the which he condemned the world, and became heir of the righteousness which is by faith" (11:7). This brief note concerning Noah and his faith gives to us another illuminating picture of faith and its effect in the life of a human being. Phillips's translation of this passage seems to set out the true meaning of the words with greater clarity: "It was through his faith that Noah, on receiving God's warning of impending disaster, reverently constructed an ark to save his household. This action of faith condemned the unbelief of the rest of the world, and won for Noah the righteousness before God which follows such a faith."

Faith is the focal point in all of these pen pictures of Old Testament believers. In every action of these men and women, faith was the motivating factor. In studying these great personalities, we should never lose sight of the element of faith. These Old Testament scenes were never intended as mere eulogies to the persons named but examples of what true faith is and what it does when it becomes a part of a person's life. The emphasis throughout the chapter is upon faith, not upon persons. We cannot, of course, completely lose sight of the person, for the person furnishes us with the modus operandi for the functions of faith. The danger is that we may lose sight of the faith which serves as the cause and inspiration for heroic conduct. Lest we lose sight of this primary emphasis upon faith, the writer of the epistle has repeated the phrase—by faith—at the introduction to each Old Testament character.

In following the influence of faith in the life of Noah, let us consider three things: the nature of Noah's faith, the visible token of Noah's faith, and the effect of Noah's faith.

The Nature of Noah's Faith

It would be safe to say that Noah had faith in God. This general statement would be true of all people of genuine faith. Faith in God is the genesis and basis of true faith. But the faith mentioned in our text was a faith which was objectified in a particular aspect of God's plan or purpose. Noah's faith had to do with a promise which God had made. It was even more specific than that—it was belief in the promise of God to destroy the world with a flood. God had forewarned Noah and had revealed to Noah His purpose to destroy the world with a flood. Noah believed that God would do just that. That is faith.

Noah was "warned of God of things not seen as yet." There was no visible sign in the sky of any such deluge, yet by faith, Noah believed that it would come to pass just as God had spoken. In this case, faith was delving into the realm of the future, making the things yet to be as sure as if they had already transpired. Faith believes the promises of God, whether they be promises of good or evil. God did give to Noah some indication as to the reason for this proposed action; however, whether any reason is given, faith accepts without question the validity of God's promises. Fortunately, God usually does not leave us completely in the dark. In most instances, He does give to us some indication of the reason for His action but not always.

In this instance, God promised to destroy the world because of gross wickedness which had swept over the populated world. The Genesis account describes it like this:

> And God saw that the wickedness of man was great in the earth, and that every imagination of the thoughts of his heart was only evil continually. And it repented the Lord that he had

made man on the earth, and it grieved him at his heart. And the
Lord said, I will destroy man whom I have created from the face
of the earth; both man, and beast, and the creeping thing, and
the fowls of the air; for it repenteth me that I have made them.
. . . And God said unto Noah, The end of all flesh is come before
me; for the earth is filled with violence through them; and behold, I will destroy them with the earth (6:5-13).

The evils of the antediluvian civilization were expressed in
many different forms, but most of it grew out of intermarriage
between believers and unbelievers. In this same sixth chapter
of Genesis, we are told that "the sons of God [descendents of
Seth] saw the daughters of men [descendents of Cain] that they
were fair; and they took them wives of all which they chose"
(v. 2). It was then that the Lord said, "My spirit shall not always
strive with man." Whenever believers and unbelievers are
linked together in any kind of intimate association, the fruit of
unbelief and evil are always predominant. Is this not one of the
grave dangers threatening the integrity of our present-day
civilization? Dr. W. A. Criswell observed: "Scarcely will there
be found in His Book anything against which the Almighty
pleads more earnestly than the intermarriage of believers and
unbelievers."[1] Then he went on to make this significant comment concerning this problem in our day:

> Herein lies one of the secrets of the building of the church and
> of the purity of the kingdom of God in the hearts of men.
> . . . If we do not make sure of the Christian foundation for our
> homes, if we do not seek Christian marriages for our young
> people, then we have no right to hope for power and purity in
> kingdom work.[2]

Just as God promised in the days of Noah that He would
destroy the world because of the prevalence of ribald and god-
less conduct, so He has promised that He will destroy the world
again. The apostle Peter has described this promise for us in his
second epistle:

> The day of the Lord will come as a thief in the night; in the

which the heavens shall pass away with a great noise, and the elements shall melt with fervent heat, the earth also and the works that are therein shall be burned up. Seeing then that all these things shall be dissolved, what manner of persons ought ye to be in all holy conversation and godliness (3:10-11).

People of faith believe this promise of God and look with frightful reverence toward that fateful day. By faith Noah believed the promise of God concerning the destruction of the world and set out to do something about it. This leads us to our second thought.

The Visible Token of Noah's Faith

Noah's faith expressed itself in a tangible way. Believing the promise, Noah set out at once to construct an ark as instructed by the Lord. Through many long and arduous days of toil, he worked on the ark, a large flat boat capable of accommodating him, his wife, his three sons and their wives, and a pair of each species of animal (Gen. 6:19-20; compare 7:2). According to instructions, Noah made only one door, and all who came in had to come through that one door. Here we have an impressive antetype of our salvation. There are many striking similarities between the ark of Noah and our salvation in Christ. But this is a subject for another study.

In keeping with our main theme of faith, the ark which Noah built was a visible token of his faith in the promise of God. While faith involves that which is invisible, it usually expresses itself in something which is tangible and visible. Faith is an investment in the unseen, but it is not much faith if it does not express itself in the realm of the seen.

For instance, faith in Christ for salvation is an invisible experience. No one can actually see another person believe in Christ. This is an experience which involves the invisible human spirit and the invisible Christ. But if that faith is genuine, it will express itself in some tangible way. Usually it expresses itself in the form of a public profession of faith, a submission to the symbol of baptism, and an identification with a local church. These are visible signs of an invisible faith. Faith without a visible sign is possible but hardly probable. Faith in Christ's word and work will usually express itself by active support of the program of the church. Noah proved his faith in the promise of God by building the ark. We also prove our faith in the promises of God by participating in the work of missions and evangelism. As James said, "Shew me thy faith without thy works, and I will shew thee my faith by my works" (2:18).

The Effect of Noah's Faith

The ark was simply the visible expression of Noah's faith. What did this expressed faith actually accomplish in the world? According to the words of our text, two things grew out of Noah's faith: By it he condemned the world, and he became heir of the righteousness which is by faith. Let us take a closer look at these two things.

In what sense did Noah's faith condemn the world? It makes little difference whether we look to his faith or to his ark as the antecedent of the relative pronoun *which*. Since the ark was the visible expression of his faith, then it must also have reference to faith. So the faith of Noah condemned the world. There are two ways to look at this. The interpretation of Weiss[3] is that Noah, by building the ark for his own rescue, showed that he considered the world doomed, thus passing judgment upon it. Others, including men like Marcus Dods[4] and J. H. Thayer,[5] interpret this part of the passage to mean that Noah's faith threw into relief the unbelief of those about him, thus pronouncing judgment upon them. When by good example a person renders another's wickedness the more evident and censurable, that person passes judgment. There was a very marked contrast between Noah's faith and its resultant conduct and the attitude and conduct of the people of the world who lived about Noah. His act of faith had pointed up the wickedness of the world as the object of God's wrath and destruction. To this day people of faith in God's salvation, by their turning away from the world, place the stigma of condemnation upon the world. By our faith, we are saying that the world is condemned, else there would be no point in our turning from it unto that which is invisible and yet real.

Noah's faith also resulted in his becoming an heir of righteousness. A more literal rendering of this part of our text would read like this: "And he became an heir of the according-to-faith righteousness" (v. 7). Two things are implied here. First, it implies that righteousness is inherited, not earned. This means that it must come from outside of ourselves. We cannot produce a righteousness in ourselves which would be acceptable to God, but we can inherit such a righteousness. To inherit something means to receive it as a gift. It is something to which we are entitled, not by works but by relation. That relation, of course, is a relation to Jesus Christ, God's Son.

In the second place, we learn that this inherited righteousness is administered through the means of faith. It is the "according-to-faith righteousness." B. F. Westcott explained that this "righteousness which 'answers to,' 'corresponds with' faith, is that righteousness which God alone can give, which answers to, corresponds with, that spiritual order which faith alone enters."[6]

God bestows righteousness as an inheritance, but not apart from faith. Noah is the first man in Genesis who is called "righteous," but the writer of this epistle is quick to explain that Noah's righteousness grew out of his faith. There are two kinds of righteousness: a so-called work-righteousness and a faith-righteousness. A work-righteousness may have some commendable features, but it is imperfect and inadequate when measured in the light of God's standards and requirements.

The only righteousness which is acceptable to God is faith-righteousness, and this is an inherited righteousness. Through faith, we believe in Christ and accept Him as our personal Lord and Redeemer; because of that faith and on the basis of it, He bestows on us a righteousness which is better than our own. It is the righteousness of Christ. The hymn writer, Edward Mote, put it like this:

> When he shall come with trumpet sound,
> Oh, may I then in him be found;
> Dressed in his righteousness alone,
> Faultless to stand before the throne.

6

The Patience of Faith

In reviewing the faith of some of the outstanding people of the Old Testament, it is not surprising to find the writer of the Epistle to the Hebrews giving more space to Abraham and those who were associated with him than to any of the other ancient believers. In a sermon on this text, Richard Watson, a nineteenth-century English preacher, said: "Among the examples of ancient faith, Abraham stood foremost. He was 'the father of the faithful;' the spiritual progenitor of the myriads of believers to the end of time."[1] Abraham's prominence in the New Testament is evidenced by the frequency of his name which appears ten times in the Epistle to the Hebrews and numerous times in the rest of the New Testament. Here are just a few examples: Acts 7:2-8; Romans 4:3; Galatians 3:6; and James 2:23.

In this comparatively lengthy review of Abraham's faith, two major features have been ably set forth in B. F. Westcott's excellent commentary on this epistle.[2] The first feature of Abraham's faith noted in our text is that of patient obedience, which is the foundation of the kingdom of God. The second is sacrifice, which is the principle of faith's development. The sacrificial aspect of Abraham's faith will be dealt with in connection with Isaac since in this respect the faith of Abraham involved also the faith of Isaac.

Throughout the passage, the author seems to have in mind the faith of the patriarchs as a whole rather than the faith of Abraham alone, though Abraham stands out as the head and leader of them all. The faith of Abraham is identified with that of Isaac, Jacob, and Joseph, and in one part of the passage (13 through 16) the use of the plural pronoun clearly points to all of the patriarchs. They are pictured in this instance as those who are looking for a "better country."

In this particular message, we shall deal with the personal or living faith of Abraham as revealed in verses 8 through 13. In the realm of faith, none has ever exceeded this patriarch of the patriarchs. He stands head and shoulders above the rest. It is no wonder that he is called the father of those who have faith. But what made the faith of Abraham so great? Our text suggests three aspects of Abraham's faith for our example and edification. His faith was marked by ready obedience, patient endurance, and contagious influence.

Ready Obedience

The most striking aspect of Abraham's faith was the ready obedience with which it expressed itself. "By faith Abraham, when he was called to go out into a place which he should after receive for an inheritance, obeyed; and he went out, not knowing whither he went" (11:8). The fuller story, of which this is but an abstract, is found in the Book of Genesis, beginning with the twelfth chapter. The abstract is confirmed by the Genesis account.

Abraham had migrated with his family from the land of his birth in Ur of the Chaldees to the city of Haran, some four hundred miles northwest up the river Euphrates. At seventy-five years of age, Abraham was called of God to leave Haran and his kinsfolk and go into a land which would be shown him. In response to this call, Abraham left Haran and came into the strange land of Canaan which God promised to him afterwards as an inheritance. This was an act of faith in the highest order. As noted in our study of Noah, faith expresses itself in obedience, but this obedience on the part of Abraham was especially significant for at least three reasons.

Without Question

First, it was without question. Nothing in this passage or in the Genesis account indicates that Abraham remonstrated with the Lord concerning this call. So far as the record goes, he did not raise a question. Under the circumstances, he might well have raised some questions; and had we been in his place, we would most likely have done so. I would not say that questions did not flash through his mind. Knowing something of human nature, I am confident that some questions must have occurred to him, but, if they did, he did not use them as arguments in dealing with the Lord concerning this call. If he had them, he must have kept them to himself.

Abraham might have raised many questions. He might have questioned the fairness of being asked to leave the people whom he had come to love as his very own. Was it right to ask him to leave a comfortable home which he had labored long to build and furnish? Why should he be asked to leave a place with which he was familiar and friends who were dear to go to a place which was completely unknown to him? Abraham certainly did not leave Haran because he had been given assurance of a land flowing with milk and honey. He had received no brochures from the chamber of commerce concerning the opportunities or beauties of the land to which he was going. The fact was that he did not even know where he was going. All he knew was that God would show it to him. With such indefiniteness, who would desire to launch out on such a journey? But in spite of all these disadvantages and uncertainties which must have run through his mind, Abraham obeyed the call of God without raising a question with God. How different is this kind of faith from that which is so often demonstrated by modern-day Christians! When we are given just a little task to perform, we are prone to question the wisdom of God and to remonstrate with Him on it. Would that we could learn to obey the calling of God without question!

Without Hesitation

Second, Abraham obeyed the call of God without hesitation. In this connection, there is an interesting grammatical construction in the original words of our text. The phrase "when he was called" (v. 8) is just one word in the Greek, a participle in the present tense. The present tense of this participle is significant. To translate literally, it would be "being called . . . Abraham obeyed"; that is, while he was being called, not some time later, he obeyed. This speaks of an unhesitating obedience to the call of God.

Even when we have no questions to raise, are we not often prone to say to the Lord when He calls, "Lord, I'll go, but let me wait until tomorrow"? Not so with the patriarch of faith. Even while the call was still ringing in his soul, he was packing for the trip. This is the kind of obedience which comes with true faith. Faith produces ready obedience, not delayed obedience. When God calls He wants us to act now, not tomorrow.

Without Reservation

Third, Abraham obeyed the call of God without reservation. He held nothing back. When he went out, he went out with all that he had—his wife, his nephew, his herds, and all his possessions. He left nothing in Haran which would keep him tied to the old place or leave him with a strong pull back to the old life. Of course, he left many relatives and friends which he must have missed and longed to see; but all that belonged to him personally, he took with him. It was a wholehearted response to God's call. When he gave himself to answer the call of God, he gave all that he had.

Our response to the call of God should follow the same pattern. When we answer the call of God to service, let us answer that call with all that we have. God is never pleased with a halfhearted response to His call. True faith holds back nothing. It responds with all or nothing. We sometimes fool ourselves into thinking that we have answered the call of God by giving only a token response to that call. Whatever God calls us to do, it deserves the dedication of all that we have to it. True faith will make just such a dedication.

Patient Endurance

To ready obedience was added patient endurance in Abraham's expression of faith. It was one thing to go out at the call of God, but another test of his faith came when he arrived in the land to which he had been led. The promise of God was not fulfilled in his entrance into the land of Canaan. There was much yet to be done before the promise would be fulfilled; therefore, it was necessary that Abraham learn the art of patient waiting. This art he did learn through faith. The writer of our epistle painted a beautiful picture of this faith as expressed in patient endurance: "By faith he sojourned in the land of promise, as in a strange country, dwelling in tabernacles with Isaac and Jacob, the heirs with him of the same promise: For he looked for a city which hath foundations, whose builder and maker is God" (11:9).

The promise, as described in our text, is very clearly a promise concerning a heavenly country, not a political or geographic one. The land of Canaan was but a symbol of the better country which God had promised. With patience Abraham and the other patriarchs had to wait for the completion of the promise.

In the realization of the promises of God, there is always the necessity of patient endurance; for these promises are seldom fulfilled immediately. They will be fulfilled to the last degree, but patient endurance through faith is required as we look toward the fulfillment of the promise. One may even die before all of the promises of God are fulfilled, but happy are those who, like Abraham, die in faith looking steadfastly and patiently toward the fulfillment which is sure to come.

Contagious Influence

A third feature of Abraham's faith was its contagious effect upon the lives of others, in particular upon the life of his wife,

Sarah. The "also" in verse 11 of our text implies to me that Sarah's faith was influenced by Abraham's faith. The Genesis account bears this out. At first Sarah and Abraham appear to have been rather skeptical with reference to her prospects of giving birth to a child. Compare Genesis 17:17 with 18:12. Nevertheless, faith won the day as Sarah caught the spirit of her faith-filled husband and began to look with confident endurance to the coming of her promised son. Through such faith, God performed a miracle, making possible the conception and birth of Isaac when Abraham and Sarah were long past the time for child bearing. Isaac's birth was a product of faith. This, in itself, is remarkable, but the point I wish to emphasize here is the influence of Abraham's faith upon others.

Some may look upon our expressions of faith with ridicule and skepticism. But when genuine faith is fully expressed, its benefits will include the inspiration to greater faith in the lives of others. True faith is contagious. In fact, this roll call of faith had as its primary purpose the stimulation of greater faith on the part of the readers. I never read these accounts of faith without feeling the surging of new faith in my own heart and life. Nor do I come in contact with Christians of notable faith that my own faith is not challenged and stimulated.

There is a twofold challenge here. There is the challenge to look around us and observe the faith of others so that our own faith will be strengthened. And it will be strengthened if we cultivate the habit of rubbing shoulders with great men and women of faith. But there is also the other challenge to give clearer expression to our own faith so that we might help to inspire greater faith in the lives of others who watch us.

Such faith as that expressed in the life of Abraham was not in vain. In fact, true faith is never in vain. Abraham conquered through faith. The story of Abraham is the story of the triumphs of faith. Abraham lived to see some of the fruit of his faith. However, much of it which he was not able to see has been made visible to persons of subsequent generations, and there is yet much fruit to be realized from Abraham's faith. But this is the way of true faith—its full benefits find fruition long after the person of faith has departed from the earthly scene. Abraham did not trust the Lord for nought, nor does anyone ever exercise faith in the Lord without fruit, some of it now, some of it later, but never in vain. Do not be afraid to trust Him with your whole heart!

7
The City of Faith

The patience of faith is revealed again in Abraham's concept of the city of faith toward which he looked. The author of Hebrews described it like this:

> These all died in faith, not having received the promises, but having seen them afar off, and were persuaded of them, and embraced them, and confessed that they were strangers and pilgrims on the earth. For they that say such things declare plainly that they seek a country. And truly, if they had been mindful of that country from whence they came out, they might have had opportunity to have returned. But now they desire a better country, that is, an heavenly: wherefore God is not ashamed to be called their God; for he hath prepared for them a city (11:13-16).

To this passage, we should add a parallel verse which is found in the thirteenth chapter of the same epistle: "For here have we no continuing city, but we seek one to come" (v. 14).

There are two analogies in this passage which are closely related and point to the same spiritual truth. The writer began by using the term "country" and closed by referring to a "city." The former is a word which may be more literally translated as "fatherland." It is a wider and more inclusive term than the latter, yet the two can hardly be separated. One can hardly think of a country or nation without thinking of the cities which serve as the great centers of population and government.

The analogy is appropriate in either case. For our purposes here, I will use the term *city*.

The comparison is between the country which now is and the country which is to come, or the city which now is and the city which is to come. The one which now is is inferior, and the one which is to come is better. It is a comparison between the present and the future, between the seen and the unseen. Faith deals with the unseen. We all know something about our present fatherland and the great cities by which it is known. Let us look at these in comparison with that city toward which we travel by faith, the city coming down from God out of heaven. We shall look first at the inferiority of our present city, then we shall be able the better to appreciate the superiority of the city of faith which is to come.

More and more, we are coming to realize that we cannot separate our nation from the cities which dot its countryside. More and more we are coming to think of life in our nation as life in our cities. We were once a rural people, but we are now a city people. The masses have increasingly gravitated to our cities. The rural areas have decreased in population while the great metropolitan areas have experienced phenomenal increases. Herein is an interesting paradox, as pointed out by Dr. G. Campbell Morgan in one of his sermons: "We are perpetually confronted in our dealing with human nature with two apparently contradictory impulses. The first is that of the gathering together of men into the life of the city; and the second is that of the ceaseless almost restless desire to be away from the city."[1] Those in the country want to move to the city, and those in the city want to go to the country, at least for the weekend. In the earlier centuries, cities arose because people needed protection against marauding and wild beasts. Plato was one of the first to make this observation concerning the origin of cities; however, Aristotle may have been closer to the truth when he suggested that the city was the outcome of the social instinct in individual life. Both factors are perhaps involved in the building of cities; however, in our modern day, we would have to say that the primary factor is economics. Most of those who turn toward the city in this era do so because of economic necessity. Opportunities for livelihood are much better now in the cities.

Regardless of the reasons, our modern civilization, especially in the country in which we live, is characterized by the prominent presence of fabulous cities with their complex systems of streets and multiple-storied buildings. They offer much that is fascinating to the physical eye and the physical appetite. But with all of their glitter, our cities are inferior in at least two respects.

First, they are full of sin and that which grows out of sin. This is not to say that there is no sin in the rural areas, but it does seem that sin is concentrated in the cities. Our newspapers tell the sordid stories of sin in its worst form in every issue, and these are paraded across our television screens. Add to this the gross immorality which is practiced in a thousand places and unreported by the press, and one gets a rather sullen picture of city life.

It would be bad enough if we should stop with the sinful act in itself, but we cannot stop there, for we must trace that sinful act to its inevitable and gruesome consequence. This would take us to the orphans' home, the hospital, the jail, the courtroom, and alas, to the funeral home. If one should dwell on these things, it could become quite depressing. With all of their glitter, our cities have become cesspools of sin and moral corruption. For this reason alone they are inferior.

But they are also inferior because they are incomplete. Our modern cities offer many conveniences. It seems that every convenience is placed within easy reach. In spite of all these conveniences, there is much left to be desired. City people are usually more dissatisfied and full of unrest than those living in the rural areas. There is more nervous tension and perplexity. Add to this the fact that our cities are never finished. Just drive through any of our modern cities, and you will see construction of some kind in nearly every block. There is never an end to it because our cities are still incomplete and unfinished. These conditions simply point up the fact that our present visible cities do not, and cannot, fulfill the deepest longing of the human heart. Therefore, we must conclude that they are inferior.

In passing, let me pause long enough to explain that I do not mean to suggest in drawing such a conclusion that those of us who live in these cities of earth should have no interest in them nor seek to improve them. We cannot ignore the cities or the nation in which we live; as Christians we should have a vital interest in the betterment of our cities and our nation. Christianity is more than just pie in the sky by-and-by. It is a life to be lived in the here and now as well as a hope for life in the sweet by-and-by. While we are here in this world, we must seek, under God's leadership, to do everything we know how to do in order to make this place a better place in which to live. There is much room for improvement. We have a Christian responsibility to be loyal to our government and to make every possible contribution within the limits of decency and order to improve the conditions under which we now live.

At the same time, we need to recognize that this is not our permanent dwelling place. We are only pilgrims and sojourners in a strange land, just as Abraham was. We look for a city which is to come, whose builder and maker is God. Some people make the mistake of neglecting their responsibility in the here and now while they dream of the city to come, but most of us have swung too far in the other direction. We act as if we think we were going to live in these earthly cities forever. True faith, as exemplified in Abraham and the patriarchs, will give to us the true perspective in this matter. The writer of Hebrews said the faithful of the Old Testament lived by faith and died in faith. By faith, they recognized that they "were strangers and pilgrims on the earth" (v. 13). They were looking for a better country; and that better country, the writer explained, was not the land from which they had come. They could easily have returned to that land had they wanted to do so. But they were looking for that heavenly city of which the earthly city is but a symbol. God did make certain promises to Abraham which can only be interpreted in terms of a physical and earthly fulfillment, such as in Genesis 15:5; 22:17; 26:4; and 32:12. The fulfillment of such promises are recognized as having been fulfilled in Israel as a nation (Num. 23:10; Deut. 1:10; 10:22; 26:5; 28:62; 1 Kings 3:8; 4:20; 2 Chron. 1:9; and Neh. 9:23). While it is evident that these Scriptures speak of a fulfillment in the physical multiplication of Abraham's posterity, I agree with Philip Edgcumbe Hughes that "the New Testament makes it plain that there is a further and ultimate fulfilment which is manifested in the spiritual lineage of Abraham; and it is in this respect that the deepest truth of the promise is to be discerned."[2]

With the same kind of faith and spiritual understanding, let us now turn toward that city which is to come to see something of its superiority over our earthly cities. Since we see it only by faith, we cannot see it in its fullest light, as we will be able to do later. But we can see it through the eyes of faith. The picture is clear enough for us to formulate some general conclusions. At least four aspects of it come into the view of faith.

A Heavenly City

First, we learn by faith that this city which is to come is not of this earth. It is a heavenly city; that is, it has a heavenly nature as over against an earthly nature. In giving to us a foregleam of this heavenly city coming down from God out of heaven, John, from the Isle of Patmos, had to use terminology which speaks of earthly values, such as gold, silver, pearl (Rev. 21). These, at least, are only inadequate symbols of the reality of that city which is to come. It will be spiritual in nature, and our present finite minds are incapable of complete comprehension. We get only a faint hint of its glory.

A City Made by God

Second, we learn by faith that this city is one whose builder and maker is God. Our earthly cities have all been built by humans, but the heavenly city will be built by God Himself. He is the architect and the contractor. It must be, therefore, so much greater than our earthly cities as God is greater than human beings. We know that, since God is sole builder of it, the heavenly city will be without all of the ugly imperfections which mar our present cities. If one can imagine one of our great cities with all of its beauty and convenience without its sin and the consequences of sin, one may understand something of what that heavenly city will be like.

A City Seen by Faith

Third, we learn by faith that this heavenly city is something which can at the moment be seen only by faith. For those who have no faith, the heavenly city will have no attraction. Since it deals in the realm of the future, it involves the element of faith, for "faith is the substance of things hoped for" (v. 1). This is the element which underlies all that is said about Abraham and the patriarchs. The city to come was real to them, not because they saw it with their physical eyes but because they saw it through the eyes of faith. A message such as this will have no meaning or appeal to the materialists, for they have no facility with which to appropriate such truth.

A Future City

Fourth, we learn by faith that the greatest consolation in the hour of death is this hope in the city which is yet to come. Abraham looked for a city which he never found in his sojourn on this earth. He died still looking for that city. As our text states, "These all died in faith, not having received the promises, but having seen them afar off, and were persuaded of them, and embraced them" (v. 13). As Leon Morris commented, "The best that happened to the saints of old was that they had glimpses of what God had for them."[3] These all died inspired, sustained, and guided by faith. They realized that the fulfillment of God's promises was not to be realized in their lives on this earth. Some of the promises would be fulfilled in the lives of their posterity which includes us, but the promise of a better city would be fulfilled in them after they had departed from this earth. Abraham had the privilege of seeing some promises fulfilled in his day; others were left for us to see; and still others remain to be seen by all in that which is yet future.

God in His wisdom and love allows us the privilege of seeing the fulfillment of some of His promises while we are still here on earth, but He reserves the fulfillment of other promises till we come into that life beyond death. The Christian life begins and continues on this earth, but it by no means ends on this earth. For the Christian, therefore, death takes on a different meaning. By faith we see beyond death. This gives us peace and courage as we approach death. A vivid picture is given to us in our text. The writer explained that these patriarchs died without having received the promises but that by faith they did see them afar and waved welcome at them at the bar of death. They "embraced" the promises at the hour of their death. This word carries the idea of greeting or saluting. It means simply that at the time of death they welcomed the vision with joy though it was far off.

Many a saint has found comfort in the dying hour by seeing afar off the coming of this heavenly city. In the light of such a vision, death became to them not a good-bye to earthly ties but a welcome into a better city. Faith works wonders throughout life, but it is never more precious than in the hour of death when it permits us to see across the river into that land which is fairer than day. I have watched people die who had not this faith, and I have seen the awful agony which expressed itself in their faces. I have also watched people die who had this faith which was so beautifully exemplified in the life and death of Abraham, and I have seen with delight the heavenly smile which seemed to possess them. A saintly mother lay on her deathbed in a local hospital. It was my privilege to visit her in her room only a few hours before she went on to be with the Lord. Never shall I forget that heavenly smile on her face as she said to me, "Pastor, I have had a glimpse of that land beyond the river; it is so beautiful; I'll soon be going there, and I am so happy!" It is this vision of the better city which is to come, a vision which belongs to those who have faith, that keeps the triumphant note in life and in death. This is what made it possible for the apostle Paul to say, "For to me to live is Christ, and to die is gain" (Phil. 1:21).

8

The Sacrifices of Faith

Dr. Marcus Dods has said that "the sacrifice of Isaac was the supreme act of Abraham's life." Then he added this explanatory sentence: "Abraham has here shown the way to the highest reach of human devotedness and to the heartiest submission to the Divine will in the most heart-rendering circumstances."[1] With this I agree.

The writer of the Epistle to the Hebrews pointed to this sacrifice of Abraham as a demonstration of faith. His commentary is brief but meaningful:

> By faith Abraham, when he was tried, offered up Isaac; and he that had received the promises offered up his only begotten son, Of whom it was said, That in Isaac shall thy seed be called: Accounting that God was able to raise him up, even from the dead; from whence also he received him in a figure (11:17-19).

The original account of this sacrifice is given in Genesis 22. Some scholars have questioned the historicity of this incident on the supposition that it is not Godlike for anyone to be divinely instructed to kill his own son and thus to be guilty of the crime of filicide for which, in our day, the penalty would be long imprisonment, death, or confinement to a mental institution. Those who so reason either deny the historicity of the record or accuse Abraham of thinking that God commanded this act when, in fact, he only thought that God commanded it.

But such an interpretation changes completely the unmistakable meaning of the simple account in the Book of Genesis.

Furthermore, there is no more reason for questioning the historicity and accuracy of this account than the account of Abraham's call and journey to Canaan. There are many highly regarded scholars who accept that account as true just as it is written. In speaking of the call of God to Abraham to sacrifice his son Isaac, Keil and Delitzsch made this significant comment:

> This word did not come from his own heart,—was not a thought suggested by the sight of the human sacrifices of the Canaanites, that he would offer a similar sacrifice to his God; nor did it originate with the tempter to evil. The word came from *Ha-Elohim,* the personal, true God, who tried him, i.e. demanded the sacrifice of the only, beloved son, as a proof and attestation of his faith.[2]

How could a righteous God command any man to perform a deed which was contrary to basic moral principles as written down in His law? This is the question which seems to disturb many. A most reasonable and satisfactory answer has been proposed by Marcus Dods in *The Expositor's Bible:*

> In the first place, Abraham did not think it wrong to sacrifice his son. . . . In Abraham's day the universal conscience had only approbation to express for such a deed as this. . . . [in the second place] We justify it precisely on that ground which lies patent on the face of the narrative—God meant Abraham to make the sacrifice in spirit, not in the outward act; He meant to write deeply on the Jewish mind the fundamental lesson regarding sacrifice, that it is in the spirit and will all true sacrifice is made. God intended what actually happened, that Abraham's sacrifice should be complete and that human sacrifice should receive a fatal blow. So far from introducing into Abraham's mind erroneous ideas about sacrifice, this incident finally dispelled from his mind such ideas and permanently fixed in his mind the conviction that the sacrifice God seeks is the devotion of the living soul not the consumption of a dead body.[3]

In these introductory observations, it should also be noted

that this incident involves the faith of Isaac as well as the faith of Abraham. Isaac enters into this picture of faith as surely as does his father, Abraham. There is no way to determine exactly how old Isaac was when he made this three days' journey up to Mount Moriah. We may surmise that he was at least approaching manhood. He carried on a sensible conversation with his father and even helped in cutting the wood for the altar fire. There is nothing to indicate that Isaac resisted when his father placed him on the altar. Had he wanted to do so he could have pulled himself loose from his father's grip, but evidently he was willing to cooperate in this venture of faith which gives evidence not only of his faith in his father but also of his faith in God. This, therefore, is a joint venture of faith. Let us not forget the faith of Isaac while we extol the faith of Abraham.

As we look at this sacrifice on Mount Moriah in the light of the interpretation given in our text, three deductions appear. To each of these let us give some serious thought.

Confirmed Faith in the Promises of God

First, it appears that this sacrifice confirmed Abraham's faith in the promises of God. There were two disturbing factors in Abraham's experience on Mount Moriah. One thing that disturbed him was the thought of having to give up his son whom he loved so dearly. The depth of his distress at the thought of giving his son must have been far greater than that which appears on the surface in reading through the account. The other thing which disturbed him was the thought of how God would fulfill His promise concerning his posterity. Without minimizing the agony that must have thrust him through at the thought of losing his son, the indications are that he was even more disturbed about God's promise than he was about losing his son. B. F. Westcott rightly observes that "the trial of Abraham was not so much in the conflict of his natural affection with his obedience to God, as in the apparent inconsistency of the revelations of the will of God which were made to him."[4]

God had promised that through Isaac, and no one else, Abraham's seed would be multiplied. "In Isaac shall thy seed by called" (Gen. 21:12). It must have been difficult for Abraham to reconcile the offering up of his son with the promise of God to multiply Abraham's descendants through Isaac. But his willingness to go on with the sacrifice is an indication of Abraham's faith in the promises of God. The true greatness of Abraham's faith is shown by his willingness to offer his son even when it appeared to contradict and nullify the promise which God had made. By faith Abraham believed that God would find a way to keep His promise even when the only means available seemed to be cut off. Even though he did not make the correct supposition concerning the manner in which God would do it (Heb. 11:19 suggests that he expected God to raise Isaac from the dead), he did express his confidence in God's ability to overcome this difficulty in order to keep His promise.

True faith never doubts the promises of God, even when it appears that they have failed. God does keep His promise. There are times when we cannot see how He is going to do it, but He always comes through in due time. Happy are those who have learned by faith to trust implicitly in the promises of God. With James Rowe they can sing:

> Darkness may o'ertake me and my song forsake me,
>   But alone I never shall be;
> For the Friend beside me promised He would guide me
>   And will keep His promise to me.

> Should misfortune meet me, friends may fail to greet me,
>   But if true to Jesus I stay
> He will still uphold me, let His love enfold me
>   Ev'ry dreary mile of the way.

> How the tho't enthralls me, that whate'er befalls me
>   One will always love me the same;
> Not a trial ever causes Him to sever
>   From the ones who honor His name.

He will keep His promise to me,
    All the way with me He will go;
He has never broken any promise spoken;
    He will keep His promise, I know.

Typified the Means of Our Redemption

Second, it appears that this sacrifice typified the means of our redemption. To the question, If God did not really intend for Abraham to give up literally his son in death, why did he ask him to go through the motions? we could answer: He wanted to test Abraham's faith, and this would be right. (It was not that God did not already know whether or not Abraham's faith was genuine, but the test was good for Abraham.) There is another answer which goes still deeper. Undoubtedly God intended by this experience to show forth the nature of our redemption, thus giving to Abraham and his people and to all future generations a symbolic picture of the basic principle underlying our redemption. Progressively this picture of redemption is revealed to us in the Old Testament. This particular picture takes us further into the understanding of redemption than anything which had been revealed in the previous chapters of Genesis.

Isaac here represents the people of this earth since he is the means through which God would multiply the seed of Abraham until it should become as the stars of the heaven and the sands of the seashore. He was bound and doomed to die by the righteous command of God, but just before the fatal blow was struck, God spoke to Abraham and pointed him to the ram which God had prepared to take Isaac's place on the altar. Isaac, therefore, was set free, not because of anything that he had done but because of the substitute which God had provided and accepted. Some have suggested that Isaac here is a type of Christ, but this cannot be. The ram which God had provided was the type of Christ. Isaac was a type of sinful and doomed humanity.

What a vivid picture of our redemption in Christ! Isaac gives to us an adequate symbol of our plight. We are doomed to die

because of our sinful nature. The knife has been drawn, and
only the thrust of the knife in a moment's action stands between us and eternal death. But God has provided a substitute.
He who knew no sin has become sin for us that we might be
made the righteousness of God in Him (2 Cor. 5:21). The Old
Testament is replete with these foregleams of redemption.
None is more significant than this one. Looking back at it from
our vantage point on the afterside of the cross, we can see in
a clearer light the intended design of this experience. Just as
God provided the ram to take the place of Isaac in order that
he might go free, so God has provided the Lamb of God to take
our place on Calvary in order that we might go free. We were
due for that fate which came upon our Lord on Calvary; but,
in order that we might be saved from it, God sent His substitute. Just as Abraham and Isaac had faith in God's provision
and accepted the offer of substitution, so we by the same kind
of faith can escape the horrors of eternal death through Jesus
Christ our substitute.

Magnified the Element of Faith

Third, it appears that this sacrifice magnified the element of
faith in victorious living. What started out to be a tragedy
ended up in victory. The difference was faith. Through faith,
Abraham returned from the mount, not with head bowed in
sorrow in the loss of his beloved son but with his face aglow in
the consciousness of victory. He had received his son back as if
it were out of death. Faith had given him the victory, even
though the victory came in a different way from that which he
had anticipated. He had accounted "that God was able to raise
him up, even from the dead" (v. 19). Indeed, he did receive him
back as if it were from the dead but only in a figure, not literally. "From whence also he received him in a figure" (v. 19). Some
expositors, like Westcott,[5] hold that the "in a figure" refers to
the birth of Isaac, explaining that Sarah was as good as dead,
so far as giving birth to offspring was concerned, when Isaac
was born. But this interpretation seems to me to be a little

unnatural. The implication is that the writer of Hebrews was thinking in terms of a receiving back which would not apply to his birth. It is more natural to take these words as referring to the receiving back of Isaac from the very jaws of death. Actually, so far as the minds of Abraham and Isaac were concerned, Isaac had already been given up as dead. The sacrifice had already been made in their own minds.

So faith brought about a victory, not the literal resurrection of Isaac out of death but a resurrection in figure which was just as glorious. It constituted a victory, and, indeed, the figure does point to a resurrection from the dead, for in Christ we are brought out of death into life.

The thought which I want to emphasize here is the glorious fact that faith always produces victory, even though that victory may not always come in the way we had anticipated. When we walk by faith, there will be times of apparent failure; but always victory will come forth right out of that apparent failure. Often the victory of faith is not something apart from the apparent failure but something which grows right out of the apparent failure. If we walk by faith, we will learn to let God give us the victory in His own way, and the way will often surprise us. But what is more surprising and glorious is the fact that Abraham and Isaac learned through experience what the apostle John taught in principle: "This is the victory that overcometh the world, even our faith" (1 John 5:4).

9
Faith and the Future

Following the more lengthy paragraph which describes the faith of Abraham, we have, in this roll call of faith, a very brief reference to the faith of the other patriarchal leaders in the line of Abraham—Isaac, Jacob, and Joseph. Isaac's faith is expressed in his blessing of Jacob and Esau "concerning things to come" (11:20). Jacob is described in his last days on earth leaning on the top of his staff (11:21). With his rapidly waning strength, he expressed his faith by blessing both the sons of Joseph in regard to things yet to come. The last picture of the patriarchs is that of Joseph in his dying hour. He talked to those at his bedside about the promised Exodus of the children of Israel out of Egypt. He expressed his faith by giving instruction concerning the reinterment of his bones in the land of his fathers. "By faith Joseph, when he died, made mention of the departing of the children of Israel; and gave commandment concerning his bones" (11:22). Leon Morris observed that all of these patriarchs had a faith that looked beyond death. Then Morris made this significant comment:

> With all three the significant thing was their firm conviction that death cannot frustrate God's purposes. Their faith was such that they were sure God would work his will. So they could speak with confidence of what would happen after they died. Their faith, being stronger than death, in a way overcame death, for their words were fulfilled.[1]

There seems to be little that is exciting about these brief

pictures of the faith of the patriarchs. The account is somewhat routine and uneventful, and yet I have detected an intimation concerning an element of faith which is both fundamental and exciting. This element is in evidence in each of these accounts dealing with the patriarchs, but it seems to be most prominent in the account of Joseph's faith. Perhaps we can best explain it by drawing three deductions, each one growing out of and explaining the previous one.

Confident Expectation

Let us observe, first of all, that Joseph's faith was the kind of faith which believed that a certain thing would take place in the future. This was more than hope; it was confident expectation. All genuine hope involves an element of faith. This thing which he expected to take place in the future was the Exodus of the children of Israel from Egypt.

Joseph had reason to believe this because God had promised it. Twice God spoke to Joseph's father, Jacob, to assure him that the children of Israel would return from Egypt. Just as he was about to go down into Egypt at the request of his long-lost son, God spoke to Jacob in this manner: "I am God, the God of thy father: fear not to go down into Egypt; for I will there make of thee a great nation: I will go down with thee into Egypt; and I will also surely bring thee up again: and Joseph shall put his hand upon thine eyes" (Gen. 46:3-4). Then again just before his death in Egypt, God reassured Jacob concerning this promise. Jacob, in turn, reassured his son Joseph with these words: "Behold, I die: but God shall be with you, and bring you again unto the land of your fathers" (Gen. 49:21). Joseph believed this promise of God coming through the lips of his father. With absolute confidence and without a hint of doubt, Joseph believed that the children of Israel would one day return out of the land of Egypt into the land of their fathers. This was a specific object on the horizon of his faith.

True Christian faith should always leave us with a sense of confidence concerning the ultimate triumph of God's purpose and plan, but there are times when faith should become more specific. One has not experienced faith in its highest form until one has come to a sense of confident expectation with reference to some particular thing. This is when faith rises to its highest level.

A Higher Level of Faith

This leads us to our second deduction. Joseph's faith was the kind of faith which acted concerning that expected thing as if it had already come to pass. Herein is the true test of that higher level of faith. It is one thing to say that one believes a certain thing will come to pass, but it is another thing to act as if that thing had already come to pass. This is where we often fail in the testing of our faith. The prophet Jeremiah expressed this kind of faith when he purchased a piece of property in his home town of Anathoth even though he knew that the Babylonians would take Judah into captivity. His faith led him to believe that Judah would return, and he acted upon that faith (Jer. 32:7-9). Faith never fails, but we often fail to prove that the faith we profess is all that we profess it to be.

True faith is always willing to act upon the belief professed. Joseph believed by faith that the children of Israel would one day leave the land of Egypt and return to the land of their fathers. On the basis of that faith, he gave instructions to him family concerning the reinterment of his bones in the land of Canaan. He did not have to say more about his faith in the Exodus. This request concerning the removal of his bones was enough to verify his faith.

We often talk about our faith, but when the real testing time comes we are not willing to act on that faith. This is the acid test. The story is told of a visitor at Niagara Falls who had just watched a tightrope walker walk calmly across a wire far above the turbulent falls. The visitor was asking the man to make another walk across the wire for the benefit of a friend who had just arrived. The man hesitated, but when the visitor insisted, he asked, "Do you really believe that I can walk across that wire again?" To this question the visitor replied, "Why, sure I believe you can walk across that wire again; I even believe that you could push a wheel-barrow across it!" The wire walker then probed the visitor's faith with this further question, "Do you really believe that I could push this wheelbarrow across that wire?" After the visitor again assured him of his confidence in his ability, the wire walker tested the visitor's faith with this simple injunction, "Well, get in, and let's go!" Whether or not this actually happened, I cannot say. It could be a fictitious story, but, even so, it still illustrates the point.

If faith is the "substance of things hoped for, the evidence of things not seen" (v. 1), then we should act as if the thing hoped for were already at hand. If we do not act in such manner, we deny the faith which we profess. Faith really knows no future, for faith makes the future as if it were the present or past. Dr. A. J. Gordon, in his beautifully written and highly inspiring little book *The First Thing in the World,* gives the following interesting distinction between love, hope, and faith:

> Love comes with full hands bringing something to God; Hope comes with outstretched hands expecting something, yet to be given from God; Faith comes with empty hands to receive something which has already been given by God. . . . Let it be distinctly recognized that Faith originates nothing; she only recognizes what is, and receives it on the soul's behalf. The opening eye did not create the lovely landscape which it pictured to the mind; it simply apprehended what was there already, and received the impress of it upon its sensitive retina, and so made an inward reality of what before was an outward fact.[2]

Dr. Gordon has reminded us here of a very important aspect of faith. In the area of faith, things future are treated as if they had already been. For that reason the natural and normal reaction to faith is conduct in keeping with that which has been brought out of the unseen into the seen or out of the future into the present. So far as Joseph was concerned, the Exodus was yet in the future; but so far as faith was concerned, it was just as sure as if it had happened yesterday; thus he acted accordingly by giving instruction concerning his bones. In the mind of God the Exodus had already happened, for it was a part of his eternal plan and purpose. Therefore, when by faith we begin to understand the mind of God we can, with all assurance, deal with these future things as if they had already happened.

This is what James meant when he discussed in his epistle the relationship of faith and works. He insisted that true faith must produce works. Faith is not faith if it does not make things so real that we act upon them as if they were physically real or presently in hand. Much of our talk about faith is little more than mere talk. We talk about our faith in the immanent return of our Lord to earth, yet we act as if we thought that return was at least a hundred years away. Is this real faith? As James put it, "Show me your faith without the works, and I will show you my faith by my works" (Jas. 2:18, NASB).

Faith and the Will of God

Now for our third deduction: Joseph's faith was based upon a conviction that this thing still to come was in keeping with the will of God. It would be foolish to exercise or act upon a faith in something yet to come if there is not some reasonable evidence that it is the will of God for it thus to come to pass. Faith has been misinterpreted and abused by those who talk of a faith which never produces action, but faith is also abused by those who recklessly launch out on adventures of so-called faith when there is no reasonable basis in the will of God. For instance, I would be foolish to act as if I were going to receive a new Cadillac automobile tomorrow when I had no reason to believe that this was in God's plan for me. Such faith would be nothing more than rank presumption.

God always honors faith on the part of His people, but we may question the reckless kind of faith which presumes on His will. There are times, however, when we have reason to believe that a certain thing is in keeping with God's will. When such reason is in evidence, faith can and should be exercised in such a way that we act as if the thing were already in the present. But we must always be careful not to presume on God, taking for granted that certain things will be done when we have no real assurance from God that they are in His will and plan for us.

Concerning many of the details of life we cannot be absolutely sure of God's will as it pertains to the future. In such cases, we must exercise our faith by being completely submissive to any route which God might choose for us, recognizing that His will is best for us no matter which direction it may lead. But there are times when we are given assurance within that a certain thing is in keeping with God's will and that it will come to pass. In such times, we should exercise our faith by acting as if the coming event were already a reality. It is at this point that faith makes the big difference. If one does have the assurance that a certain thing is of God, one should be ready to demonstrate one's faith by acting as if it had already happened.

It has been reported that once the great preacher Charles Haddon Spurgeon[3] called a meeting in his study of a group of Christian friends to pray concerning some definite needs in the orphanage program which was sponsored by his church. So keenly did he feel that it was God's will for these orphans to be fed and so strong was his faith in this conviction that when it came time for the last man to pray, Spurgeon said, "Now, brother, you thank the Lord for answering our prayer!" This is faith in action. He was so deeply convinced of a forthcoming supply that he could thank the Lord as if it were already in hand. This, of course, would be rank presumption if we acted like this in reference to any or every little whim which might suit our fancies. However, when it involves a matter which we know to be in keeping with God's will, faith leads us to act as if it had already happened. Though the supply had not already been received, in the mind of God it had already been granted.

By faith Spurgeon simply discovered and interpreted the mind of God in such a way that the thing to come was as real as if it had already come. This is the kind of faith Joseph had. It is the kind we need.

10
Faith and Vision

From the patriarchs, we turn rather abruptly to Moses in our review of the heroes of faith as delineated by the writer of the Epistle to the Hebrews in this eleventh chapter (vv. 23-28). It is not surprising to find the author giving considerable space to the faith of Moses. One who played such an important role in the history of the Hebrews would naturally come into the picture of faith with commensurate prominence. The basic facts in the life of Moses are of such familiarity that we need not make a detailed review at this point. We will have occasion throughout this discussion to refer to some of the more familiar events in the life of Moses. Let us pause long enough to remind ourselves that it is not Moses himself who is to hold the spotlight in this discussion, but his faith. Moses comes into the picture as a demonstrator of faith.

From the brief sketch which we have in our text, the faith of Moses is outstanding in three areas. Whether in Moses or in a twentieth-century Christian, true faith will express itself in some degree in these three ways. We will do well, therefore, to ponder carefully these three features of the faith of Moses.

Possibilities in People

First, Moses' faith made it possible for him to see possibilities in people which others could not see. This feature of the faith is demonstrated not only in Moses but also in his parents. By faith Moses' parents saw in the child Moses something unusual. The Scripture says only that "they saw he was a proper child"

(v. 23). The word "proper" carries literally the idea of being "comely" or "beautiful." In reviewing this same incident in a sermon before the Sanhedrin, Stephen referred to the child Moses as being "exceeding fair" (Acts 7:20). Stephen used the same Greek word as that which appears in our text, except that it is followed in the Greek with the prepositional phrase "to God." The obvious idea is that the child appeared to be unusually beautiful or proper in relation to God and God's purpose in the world. This is to say that the parents recognized by faith that God had some specially important mission for him to perform in the world. B. F. Westcott observes that "faith under two forms moved the parents of Moses to preserve him. Something in his appearance kindled hope as to his destiny; and then looking to God for the fulfilment of His promise they had no fear of the king's orders."[1]

With this same kind of faith, Moses recognized that the poor slave people in Egypt were "the people of God" (v. 25). Even though they were bound in a slavery of the worst kind, he recognized by faith that these enslaved people were destined to play an important role in God's kingdom. To him they were not a hopelessly enslaved race; they were the people of God.

There are many other examples of such faith. Jesus looked upon the impulsive and vacillating Simon and referred to him as Peter, the rock. There were times when it appeared that Jesus had misnamed Simon, but Jesus looked by faith into the time to come. Therefore, He could see in Peter what others could not see. Faith gives an insight into the potential which is in a person. By faith, Christian men and women have worked untiringly and hopefully with boys and girls who seemed to be incorrigibles. They often live to see, even if after long and anxious years of working and waiting, their faith blossom forth in beautiful flower. By faith one can look into the inner recesses of an otherwise unbecoming life to see a potential Moses, Paul, Peter, Luther, Spurgeon, or Truett.

The story is told of a Nonconformist believer in England toward the close of the eighteenth century who, when all others had given up, kept coming back to minister to a young man who worked in a cobbler's shop. The believer's faith had convinced him that God had something special in store for this seemingly unpromising lad. Finally his efforts began to show forth fruit. The lad was converted. Then began a long, eventful, and fruitful career in the service of the Lord as a pioneer missionary to India, laying the foundation for a great missionary program which is gaining momentum with every passing year. This lad was William Carey, the father of modern missions.[2]

Some of the greatest leaders among us today in the cause of Christ are men who at one time were given up by some as hopeless delinquents, but thanks be unto God for men and women of faith who saw in them more than others saw and who manifested their faith by their unceasing efforts to bring out this hidden potential. Moses had this kind of faith.

Properly Evaluate Situations

Second, Moses' faith made it possible for him to evaluate properly situations which others could not evaluate. By faith he was able to see the inferiority of a seemingly pleasant situation and the superiority of a seemingly undesirable situation.

> By faith Moses, when he was come to years, refused to be called the son of Pharaoh's daughter; Choosing rather to suffer affliction with the people of God, than to enjoy the pleasures of sin for a season; Esteeming the reproach of Christ greater riches than the treasures in Egypt: for he had respect unto the recompence of the reward. By faith he forsook Egypt, not fearing the wrath of the king: for he endured, as seeing him who is invisible (11:24-27).

Here are two situations. One involves the comforts, conveniences, scholastic advantages, prestige, and wealth of Egypt. The other involves the toil, suffering affliction, deprivation, and shame of a condition of abject slavery. For those who are of this world and who have no faith, there would be no need for a second thought in the matter of choice between the two. Everything points to the former as the desirable situation, and there is nothing in the latter which could be in any way attractive. According to the view of the world, one would be something less than a fool who would choose the latter over the former. But faith can see and evaluate a situation in ways which are unknown and inexplicable to those who live by sight.

It is not that people of faith are blind to reality or reason. On the contrary, faith gives an added sense of reality and reason. Time has revealed and will reveal that the evaluations of faith are superior and sound. This particular choice of Moses was not a hasty choice or one that was made in the immaturity of childhood. It was made after he had become a full-grown man and had had ample opportunity to study the situations. W. M. Taylor makes this interesting comment on Moses' choice:

> That the choice of Moses was not blindly made in the impulsive ardor of boyhood, and while yet he knew not what he was required either to suffer or to sacrifice, but maturely, when he was come to years, and was in the full vigor of his powers; that it involved the forfeiture of the grandest position in the world, and the endurance of privation and hardship; that it was made from a regard to truth and with firm belief in the rightness of God's moral administration and in the certainty of a future recompense; and that it resulted in the attainment of a nobler sort even of earthly grandeur than he could otherwise have reached, with the added advantages of the favor of God and eternal glory.[3]

By faith Moses was able to see the folly of enjoying the pleasures of sin for a season. He did understand that there were pleasures in sin. No one can be realistic and deny that there are no pleasures to be enjoyed in the sins of this world. Moses did not turn from the sinful life of Egypt because there were no pleasures to be found in such a life. Neither does one turn now from the sins of the world because there are no pleasures in them. The difference lies in the nature of these pleasures. Faith gives to one the ability to see that the pleasures of sin are "for a season." Without faith one sees only the pleasure which is present.

Faith is not blind to these pleasures of sin, but it goes beneath and behind the pleasures to see what does not usually show up on the surface. In his exposition of this text Dr. W. M. Taylor has pointed out four defects in the pleasures which grow out of sin.[4] First, they are short-lived; second, they leave a sting behind and will not bear after reflection; third, they are such that the oftener they are enjoyed the less enjoyment there is in them; and fourth, they are most expensive. Dr. Taylor is right on each score. These are the things which Moses doubtlessly saw when he looked through the eyes of faith. These are also the things which we will see when we look at the world through the eyes of faith. We cannot deny that the pleasures are there, but we can see that the pleasures are overshadowed by other and more objectionable features. History stands as an ever-present reminder of the grim reality of these obnoxious features of the pleasures of sin. The poet was speaking of worldly pleasures when he said:

> Pleasures are like poppies spread:
> You seize the flow'r, its bloom is shed;
> Or like the snow falls in the river,
> A moment white—then melts for ever;
> Or like the borealis race,
> That flit ere you can point their place;
> Or like the rainbow's lovely form
> Evanishing amid the storm.

But faith not only brings out the obnoxious features of the pleasures of sin; it also reveals the true glory of that which appears to be unattractive at the moment. On the surface, the pleasures of sin far outshine the suffering of affliction in the service of Christ. But again faith takes us behind the scenes and shows us things which cannot be seen with the naked eye. It shows us that ultimately these afflictions only add to our stature and prepare us for better and more enduring pleasures.

The world can never understand why Christians will dedicate their lives to a service which is characterized by hardship, sacrifice, and vilification. People of faith can understand because they can see things which the world can never see. They can see that the benefits of faithful and sacrificial service to Christ are more precious and more valuable in the end than all the short-lived pleasures of worldly living. Moses had "respect unto the recompence of the reward" (v. 26). He looked through the eyes of faith down the corridors of time to see that the ultimate rewards are much greater for those who follow the path of reproach in the service of God.

Recognize a Means of Redemption

Third, Moses' faith made it possible for him to recognize a means of redemption which others could not recognize. It was by faith that Moses "kept the passover, and the sprinkling of blood, lest he that destroyed the firstborn should touch them" (v. 28). It would be presumptuous to say that Moses understood the true meaning of the Passover as clearly as we do who live in this Christian era; however, through faith Moses was able to see in that Passover celebration far more than others of lesser faith were able to see. He could see in the slaying of the lamb and the sprinkling of the blood a symbol of deliverance. Because of that, he established the ritual as a permanent part of the Jewish religious system. He did this because he knew by faith that it had a tremendous symbolic significance. He sensed that there was deliverance in the sacrifice of the innocent lamb not only for the nation as a whole but also for each individual as well.

The same kind of faith makes it possible for us to look back to that Passover in which Jesus was sacrificed as the Lamb of God and see in it our only hope of deliverance from the condemnation of sin. To the world this makes very little sense. In fact, the idea of the shedding of blood is repulsive to those who have no faith. A woman once told me that she liked our church and the Christian religion in its ethical expressions, but the idea of the shedding of the blood of Christ for our redemption was repulsive to her more aesthetic tastes.

Faith sees the shedding of the blood of Christ in a different light. Instead of an ugly, uncultured sight, faith looks upon the cross of Christ to see the dying of the Son of God as our only hope for deliverance. It does take some faith to see this; however, once a little faith is exercised, the faith itself grows stronger, and the meaning of the death of Christ becomes more precious. It is not the idea that any one delights in seeing the Son of God afflicted and crucified, but it is the idea that this is an expression of God's love for us and the only way by which we could ever have any hope for the world to come. It is by faith, therefore, that we glory in the Paschal Lamb which was slain on the cross. It is by faith that we are able to sing with John Bowring:

> In the cross of Christ I glory,
> Tow'ring o'er the wrecks of time,
> All the light of sacred story
> Gathers round its head sublime.

> When the woes of life o'ertake me,
> Hopes deceive and fears annoy,
> Never shall the cross forsake me:
> Lo! it glows with peace and joy.

> When the sun of bliss is beaming
> Light and love upon my way,
> From the cross the radiance streaming
> Adds new luster to the day.

> Bane and blessing, pain and pleasure,
> By the cross are sanctified;
> Peace is there that knows no measure,
> Joys that thro' all time abide.

In one sense the cross of Christ is history's ugliest scene, and yet when viewed with the eyes of faith it becomes history's most glorious incident. The ignominy of the cross can never be blotted completely out; yet when we look at that cross through the eyes of faith, a beam of light shines forth revealing God's way for our salvation. This beam of light Moses saw dimly when he looked at the shed blood of the lamb in the Passover ceremony; how much more shall we see it who now walk by faith and not by sight!

11
Faith and Miracles

In Hebrews 11:29, there is a change from the singular pronoun to the plural. The preceding verses tell of the faith of Moses, but now the writer turned to the faith of the people as a whole. Before, it was "he" who did thus and so by faith; now it is "they" who did thus and so by faith. The faith of the people is demonstrated in two miraculous events: the crossing of the Red Sea on dry land and the falling of the walls of Jericho. This brief picture of the faith of the people suggests three thoughts for our consideration.

Reflected Their Leaders' Faith

In the first place, we observe that their faith was a reflection of their leaders' faith. The leader, of course, was different in each of the two incidents mentioned. In the crossing of the Red Sea, Moses was the leader; in the conquest of Jericho, Joshua was the leader. It makes little difference which leader we consider here, for they were both of the same calibre in this matter of faith. Both were outstanding men of faith.

People usually reflect the faith and attitude of their leader. The leader, of course, cannot and does not answer for the people in matters of faith and religion. The people must answer for themselves individually, but a group of people are usually found to reflect the attitude of their leader. People will seldom rise any higher than their leader. The faith of any leader is contagious; so also is his faithlessness. The people of Israel in a time of crisis exercised faith because they saw that faith expressed in their leaders.

This places a heavy responsibility upon the leader. The faith of leaders affects not only their own personal lives but also the lives of all those who come under the scope of their leadership. Everyone has some influence upon someone else, but this influence is multiplied and intensified in the case of the leader. For this reason, leadership is so vitally important in any area of endeavor. Generally speaking, people are gregarious, that is, they have a tendency to flock together and to do things together. And what they do together is usually determined by the leader. Every person carries within a solemn responsibility in matters of faith and religion, but the person who leads seems to carry a double responsibility in these things.

At times people are bad in spite of good leadership; but in most instances, people reflect the character of their leader. People unconsciously absorb the attitudes and habits of their leader. For instance, a church whose pastor is friendly will usually be recognized as a friendly church. By the same token, a church whose pastor is outstanding in faith will also be outstanding in faith. There were times when the people of Israel rebelled against the leadership of Moses and did things which were not in keeping with his character or spirit, but most of them in the time of crisis emulated the example of their great leader. This was also true under the equally effective leadership of Joshua. In fact, Joshua became what he was largely because of the influence of Moses under whose leadership he grew up. The prophet Hosea was right in saying "like people, like priest" (Hos. 4:9). There will always be exceptions, but, in the main, any particular group of people will reflect what they see in their leader. When people are faithless, it will usually be found that the leader was also faithless. When people express faith and optimism, it will usually be found that the leader is outstanding in faith. It is almost impossible to separate the spirit of a people from the spirit of their leader. While it is true that every individual must give a personal account unto God, most individuals are influenced in their thinking and attitudes by their leaders. What a sobering thought for those of us who try to lead! The people of Israel would never have launched out by faith to cross the Red Sea had it not been for the presence and inspiration of their great leader Moses. Nor would they have continued by faith to walk around the city of Jericho until the walls fell had it not been for the presence and inspiration of their great leader Joshua.

Accompanied by Visible Signs

In the second place, we observe that their faith was accompanied by visible signs. This is not a new thought, for we have observed such visible signs accompanying the faith of all of these Old Testament saints who are mentioned in this roll call. But I cannot pass this incident without calling attention to this aspect of faith again. In the case of the Israelites at the Red Sea, their faith was expressed in their willingness to walk on out into the sea even though there was the possibility the waters could return to drown them. It was not enough just to believe that the waters had been divided. They had to exercise their faith by walking across the path which had been made for them. In the incident at Jericho, their faith was expressed in their continuing to march around the city for seven days. Without faith, they would surely have given up after one day. But they kept marching for seven days. That was an evidence of their faith, a visible sign. There may have been a few to drop out of the march, though we are not told of any, but the people as a whole expressed their faith in this visible form by continuing to march through the seven days.

Faith always has its visible signs. In the absence of some visible sign, one might well suspect the absence of faith. Faith must express itself, and the signs will be forthcoming if the faith is genuine.

Resulted in Miraculous Events

In the third place, we observe that their faith resulted in miraculous events. I would not say that faith always results in a miracle, but often it does. In these two instances, faith resulted in miracles. One miracle was the parting of the waters of the Red Sea; the other was the falling of the walls of Jericho without any apparent physical force. Some interpreters, of course, have labored long at the task of "explaining away" these miracles. There are many different versions, but the end result is usually a denying of the miraculous element. Some of the explanations are quite interesting as well as fantastic. One such explanation suggests that the Israelites came upon the Red Sea at a place where it was rather wide and very shallow, so shallow that in a dry season such as this was, one could cross by foot without much difficulty. But this explanation would hardly account for the fact that the Egyptians were drowned at this same spot soon after the Israelites had crossed over.

Others have suggested some natural but rather unusual conditions which made possible the traversing of the sea as on dry ground. The Scripture itself tells us that God did use some natural means such as a strong east wind (Ex. 14:21). Whether the miracle was in the literal dividing of the waters or in the unusual force of the east wind makes little difference. In either case, a miracle was performed. If we accept the account as it is written in the Scripture, we must acknowledge that a miracle of some kind had been performed. There is no other way to explain the crossing of the Israelites on dry ground and the drowning of the Egyptians immediately thereafter.

In like manner, attempts have been made to explain away the miracle of the falling down of the walls of Jericho. Some have suggested that it was caused by a mighty earthquake which happened to strike at the very moment the Israelites had encircled the city the seventh time on the seventh day. Even if this were true—and it is a possibility—a miracle would be involved in the timing. It was a miraculous event looking at it from any point of view.

Here we are brought face-to-face with the subject of the reality of miracles and the relationship of faith to them. A miracle, according to Webster, is "an event or effect in the physical world deviating from the known laws of nature, or transcending our knowledge of these laws." People of the biblical period seemed to have no difficulty in accepting the fact of miracle. And in all of the ages since the biblical period there have been those who have shared this belief in miracles, that is, the divine suspensions of the ordinary course of nature. Like Luther, many Christians hold that God had caused visible miracles in the early stages of Christianity to foster belief in it and that these, subsequently proving unnecessary, were replaced by the far greater invisible spiritual miracles wrought by the Spirit of God.

Others, however, have challenged the reality of "so-called" miracles as recorded in the Bible and have even denied the possibility of miracles. Men like Spinoza, Hume, and Strauss[1] have attacked the idea of miracle and have given what they believed to be proofs of the impossibility of such. Many theologians, both of the present and the past, have been influenced by them.[2] Harry Emerson Fosdick, for instance, declared that miracles are considered to be "indissolubly associated with ancient ignorance and as vanishing when intelligence arrives."[3]

In spite of these influences, people of faith still believe in miracles and accept the miraculous accounts found in the Bible as credible and trustworthy. Faith recognizes God who, as sovereign over His creation, is able to do anything He desires with it. In discussing the purpose of God and the Christian life, Dr. Fred Fisher declares that "a denial of the possibility of miracle is a denial of God's control of nature."[4] C. A. Beckwith, in *The New Schaff-Herzog Encyclopedia,* explained that there are three classes of miracles: "the constant miracle of the revelation of God; the operation of God in purely natural and orderly events of human life; and the revelation of God by irregular natural phenomena at a specific period."[5] Usually thoughts concerning miracles are confined to the latter two, but the fact that a sovereign God should reveal Himself to humanity is in itself a miracle of greater proportions than those involving nature. Every experience of conversion is a miracle of God.

Faith and miracles have always been companions. They can live in the same mind or heart without difficulty. When one is absent, usually the other is absent also. Neither can live long by itself in any human mind. This is not to say that one who has faith may experience a miracle at anytime one may so desire. There are miracles in the spiritual realm which happen frequently in the lives of people who have faith, but in the area of the physical, miracles are not performed just to satisfy the whims of the human mind. One thing is sure—God does not respond to the cry of faith for a miracle just for the sake of demonstrating or displaying that faith. The so-called faith healers have abused faith at this point. In the name of faith, they have proposed to work miracles just to show off the power of their faith. God does not honor such spurious faith, notwithstanding the apparent demonstrations. Some of these demonstrations are little more than sleight-of-hand tricks or psychological maneuverings. We must confess that not all that appears to be miraculous is miraculous. This does not mean, however, that there are not genuine miracles or that God is not able to perform such miracles. We must remember that miracles have redemptive significance.

Though physical phenomena are less frequent now than in earlier centuries, we must not conclude that the miracles recorded as having taken place in those earlier centuries were not real or that God is incapable of performing such miracles even now. God has His own reasons for His use or nonuse of this miraculous power. Perhaps Luther was close to the truth in his explanation. The explanation of Dr. Fred Fisher is similar:

> Miracles are used of God to authenticate his messengers and to lead man to accept that which is new in his redemptive pro-

gram. Perhaps this explains why miracles are no longer a part of the Christian ministry. There is no redemptive purpose to be achieved by them. Our ministry is authenticated today by its harmony with the teachings of the New Testament. We have accepted a canon of measurement for any Christian message; we have no need for miracles. We need not be surprised if none are performed; it would be more surprising if any were.[6]

As for me, I believe in the God of miracles. By faith I accept as genuine the accounts of miracles which are recorded in the Bible. By faith I accept the idea that God is able to perform any kind of a miracle at anytime. By faith I have experienced a miracle in my own heart, a miracle of resurrection. I was dead in trespasses and in sins, but when I yielded my heart to Christ in faith, He brought me out of death into life. This is the greatest miracle known to human beings, but it can never be known or experienced apart from faith. By faith I believe that God can and will work a miracle through me or in my presence whenever it is expedient to accomplish His purpose in me and in the world. By faith I believe that God can work a miracle in your heart this moment, if you will but let Him in by faith. Yes, faith does result in a miracle! The testimony of John W. Peterson is the testimony of every truly redeemed soul:

> My Father is omnipotent,
>   And that you can't deny;
> A God of might and miracles,
>   'Tis written in the sky.
>
> Though here His glory has been shown,
>   We still can't fully see;
> The wonders of His might—His throne,
>   'Twill take eternity!
>
> The Bible tells us of His pow'r
>   And wisdom all way through;
> And every little bird and flow'r
>   Are testimonies, too.

It took a miracle to put the stars in place,
   It took a miracle to hang the world in space;
But when He saved my soul, cleansed and made me whole,
   It took a miracle of love and grace.[7]

12
Faith and the Past

Except for the listing of several Old Testament characters in a group, the roll call of faith closes with a reference to Rahab the harlot. We are at first shocked to find the writer of the epistle naming such a woman to receive a place along side Abraham and Moses in faith's hall of fame. But this is no mistake, oversight, or misplaced judgment. It is most appropriate and significant, as we shall see in a closer look at all of the factors involved. B. F. Westcott made this interesting observation: "The list of the champions of Faith whose victories are specially noticed is closed by a woman and a Gentile and an outcast. In this there is a significant foreshadowing of its essential universality."[1]

The exposition of the text will be developed along three lines of thought: the background of Rahab's faith, the essence of Rahab's faith, and lessons from Rahab's faith.

The Background of Rahab's Faith

Rahab's faith is all the more remarkable when we consider the background out of which it came. Her faith had to overcome three serious handicaps. First of all, she was a woman. In the day in which she lived, women were hardly noted for any thing, much less faith. Men stood in the foreground. For a woman to arrive at a place of faith comparable to that of Abraham and Moses, she would have to excel far beyond the ordinary.

In the second place, Rahab was a Gentile who knew little, if anything, of the experiences of Israel. She grew up in an environment of paganism and polytheism. It is most unusual to find a person who has grown up in that kind of an environment embracing the idea of one God. She had little opportunity for teaching or training in the art of faith in one God.

In the third place, she had long been engaged in a profession which was held in contempt by the true worshipers of Yahweh. She was a prostitute. There was little if anything in this kind of life which would be commensurate with faith in a God of holiness and righteousness. Looking at her background from these three points of view, we are all the more surprised to find her expressing faith in Israel's God. Though it appears to be ever so improbable, the fact remains as a part of the reliable record of the Word of God that she was a woman whose depth of faith has become an inspiration to all generations.

The Essence of Rahab's Faith

We have no detailed record of how Rahab came to her decision of faith. It is unlikely that she knew anything about Israel's God before the Israelites encamped across the river from her city. Reports had doubtless reached the city of Jericho concerning the exploits of these children of Israel not long after they set up camp across the river, but it is doubtful that Rahab knew very much about these people and their God until she met the spies who came to her house.

Joshua was a shrewd and intelligent general. He sensed the wisdom of spying out the land, especially the walled city which lay just across the river, before sending his armies in for conquest. He called in two of his most trusted men and sent them out to survey the situation. They perhaps went under cover of night across the river and appeared the next morning at the gate of the city disguised as merchants of some kind. They found entrance into the city without much difficulty, but soon after entering the city someone reported to the king the presence of these two suspicious-looking men who might well be spies from the Israelite camp.

Immediately the two spies sought a place of lodging. It so

happened that they found it in the home of Rahab. Perhaps she operated a boardinghouse or hostelry as a cover-up for her nefarious trade in prostitution. What these two men told Rahab we are not told, but we may reasonably suppose that they soon learned that they could confide in her. They must have told her about God's blessings and guidance through the wilderness experiences. She was obviously impressed with their story and soon became a believer in their God. God Himself must have prepared her heart for this hour.

It was reported to the king that these men had found lodging at the home of Rahab, whereupon he sent soldiers to pick up the men. Upon arriving at the home of Rahab, they were told that the men had just left the house and if they would hasten in a certain direction they would surely overtake them. The soldiers, at the suggestion of Rahab, hastened in the direction indicated in hope of overtaking the spies. Their pursuit was in vain, for Rahab had hidden the two spies on her rooftop under the flax which she had stored there.

Under cover of night, Rahab let the two spies down over the wall with a scarlet cord, but not before she had evoked from them a promise to save her and her family from destruction when the Isralites came to conquer. In order that the promise might be kept without mistake, it was agreed that she would hang a piece of this scarlet cord from her window. When the Israelites did come in to conquer the city, Rahab and her family were saved from the destruction which came upon the city.

This is the story as recorded in the Old Testament. Now we must ask: When was it in Rahab which merited such favor on the part of the people of Israel? She certainly did not deserve such treatment on the basis of her moral standing. Even though she did spare the lives of the two spies, she could certainly not be commended in the eyes of God for telling a lie. She did lie about the spies when the soldiers came to her house. We must not interpret this tribute to her faith in the Book of Hebrews to mean that God endorsed her lying about the spies. A lie is always an abomination unto the Lord and can never be thought of in any other light. God did not honor and bless her because she lied; rather, He honored and blessed her in spite of her lie. The basis of her commendation is to be found in the fact that she recognized Israel's God as the only true God.

This was the essence of her faith. She expressed faith in Israel's God and acted accordingly. She did tell a lie in order to protect the spies, but God overruled that lie to make it turn out for good. That does not mean that He endorsed it or was pleased with it. He was pleased with Rahab's faith in Him—a faith which involved action as well as words. In this manner, she gave expression of a genuine faith in God and was willing to make any sacrifice in order to become identified with those who worshiped this God. This is faith in its purest form.

Lessons from Rahab's Faith

Many lessons can be gained from a study of this interesting woman of Old Testament history. I mention only three which seem to stand out. First, true men or women of faith may be found in the most unlikely circumstances. We must admit that most people of faith grow up in an atmosphere of faith. We cannot emphasize too much the importance of providing such an atmosphere for our children. However, it is also true that once in a while there will appear a giant of faith out of a most unfavorable condition or environment.

This means that we should never scratch anyone off as incorrigible or impossible. Who knows but what that most unlikely prospect may become the shining example of faith for all of us! We confess that we are surprised to find such faith in a woman like Rahab, but our surprise only confirms the lesson that on some occasions God raises up a champion of faith right out of the den of Satan. Rahab came out of a life of harlotry to become a devoted servant of the Lord.

The story of Rahab is a tribute to the possibilities of every human soul. No one sinks so low as to be beyond the lifting power of God's grace. Jesus must have had people like Rahab in mind when He rebuked the Pharisees by saying, "Verily I say unto you, That the publicans and the harlots go into the kingdom of God before you. For John came unto you in the way of righteousness, and ye believed him not: but the publicans and the harlots believed him: and ye, when ye had seen it, repented not afterwards, that ye might believe him" (Matt. 21:31).

Most of the great people of faith whom I know were nurtured in atmospheres of faith, but a few of the most outstanding people of faith came out of dark backgrounds. These shine forth as beacon lights in a darkened world and stand as tributes to God's grace and power. Such a man was Mel Trotter who came out of the gutter of sin to become a blessing to thousands through his ministry of mercy to the downtrodden of the cities.

Our second lesson follows naturally—true faith is not determined or dependent upon one's past life. In one of his scintillating expositions on Bible personalities, the gifted preacher Clarence Macartney had this to say about Rahab: "To humble our pride and to teach us that we are saved by the grace of God, God took a harlot and by her teaches us the meaning of faith."[2] Grace and faith go hand in hand; they are inseparable. One cannot be had without the other. Faith, therefore, is not determined by the goodness of one's moral character. In fact it has no real connection with one's past record. Faith is for the present and the future. It never looks back; it always looks up and ahead. The past makes no difference, else Rahab would have had no chance. Nor would any of us have a chance were our faith determined by our past moral character and conduct.

Nor is there any contradiction to this truth in the words of James about Rahab: "Likewise also was not Rahab the harlot justified by works, when she had received the messengers, and had sent them out another way?" (Jas. 2:25). This question was raised in connection with his discussion of faith and works. It was not a question of making a distinction between faith and works or of pitting one against the other. On the contrary, he was showing the compatibility of faith and works. He was showing that Rahab proved her faith by doing something about it.

Faith which does not act is something less than faith. Rahab had genuine faith, and she proved it by what she did in caring for the spies. Her faith had nothing to do with her previous works in the realm of prostitution. Nor does our faith have anything to do with our previous works, be they good or evil.

Now for our third and final lesson—true faith brings one into the company of the great. Rahab was a disreputable harlot, but through faith she gained a place alongside of men like Abraham, Moses, and David. Faith makes the great humble and the humble great. Through faith Rahab was lifted from the harlot's den to a place in the earthly lineage of our Lord Jesus Christ. Tradition has it that Salmon was one of the two spies who found refuge in the house of Rahab. If this be true, there must be a beautiful but hidden story of romance here. We are told in Matthew 1:5 that Rahab was the wife of Salmon and mother of Boaz. This would make her the great grandmother of David. Twice she is referred to in the New Testament as an example of faith, once in this eleventh chapter of Hebrews and once in James.

In the story of Rahab, we have a tribute to the power of faith. The fruit of faith is always a noble life, regardless of past character or conduct. Let me close this meditation with these timely words from the pen of Clarence MacCartney:

> Considering the time, the place, the hour, the circumstances, and that it was a harlot who made it, this is one of the most remarkable confessions of faith in the Bible. And it is not strange that, ages after, the faith that inspired it is spoken of along with that of Abraham and Moses and Enoch and Noah.[3]

13
The Achievements of Faith

The writer of the Epistle to the Hebrews started out giving
a review of Old Testament persons to show what place faith
held in their lives. After having made mention of Abel, Enoch,
Noah, Abraham, Sarah, Isaac, Jacob, Joseph, Moses, Joshua,
and Rahab, he realized that it would take too much time and
space to finish the review; therefore, he closed the chapter with
a bare mention of a few other persons and a summary statement of the significance of faith in the lives of all of these Old
Testament notables. The summary is as follows:

And what shall I more say? for the time would fail me to tell
of Gedeon, and of Barak, and of Samson, and of Jephthae; of
David also, and Samuel, and of the prophets: Who through faith
subdued kingdoms, wrought righteousness, obtained promises,
stopped the mouths of lions, Quenched the violence of fire, escaped the edge of the sword, out of weakness were made strong,
waxed valiant in fight, turned to flight the armies of the aliens.
Women received their dead raised to life again: and others were
tortured, not accepting deliverance; that they might obtain a
better resurrection: And others had trial of cruel mockings and
scourgings, yea, moreover of bonds and imprisonment: They
were stoned, they were sawn asunder, were tempted, were slain
with the sword: they wandered about in sheepskins and goat-
skins; being destitute, afflicted, tormented; (Of whom the world
was not worthy:) they wandered in deserts, and in mountains,
and in dens and caves of the earth. And these all, having obtained a good report through faith, received not the promise:

God having provided some better thing for us, that they without
us should not be made perfect (11:32-40).

Here we have a summary of the achievements of faith.
Though the names are not mentioned, we can identify some of
the people whom the writer must have had in mind when
describing various achievements of faith. For instance, Daniel
was the one for whom the mouths of lions were closed (Dan.
6:22). The three Hebrew children "quenched the violence of
fire" (Dan. 3:26-27). Women who "received their dead raised to
life again" must have included the woman of Zarephath (1
Kings 17:9-24) and the Shunammite (2 Kings 4:17-36). Tradition has it that the prophet Isaiah was "sawn asunder." Others
are not so clearly identified, but we are certain that for every
achievement the writer had some Old Testament person or
persons in mind.

These achievements of faith are of two kinds: those in the
realm of actual accomplishment and those in the realm of patient endurance. These two main divisions of the achievements
of faith will form the two main divisions of our interpretation
of this passage. First we shall consider what faith enables us to
accomplish; then we shall consider what faith enables us to
endure.

What Faith Enables Us to Accomplish

Faith is both active and passive. The people of the Old Testament had both kinds, and we need both kinds. We need the kind
of faith that will spur us on to accomplish worthwhile goals. We
also need the kind of faith that will cause us to be patient and
steadfast in the face of tribulations. True faith has both characteristics.

In the realm of actual accomplishment, we have three sets of
triplets which show up in our text. These have been detected
and arranged by B. F. Westcott in this manner:[1]

The first triplet describes the broad results which believers
obtained:

Material victory ["subdued kingdoms"].
Moral success in government. ["wrought righteousness"].
Spiritual reward ["obtained promises"].
The second triplet notices forms of personal deliverance from:
Wild beasts ["stopped the mouths of lions"].
Physical forces ["Quenched the violence of fire"].
Human tyranny ["escaped the edge of the sword"].
The third triplet marks the attainment of personal gifts:
Strength ["out of weakness were made strong"].
The exercise of strength ["waxed valiant in fight"].
The triumph of strength ["turned to flight the armies of the aliens"].

Then follows one climactic note in the accomplishments of faith: "Women received their dead raised to life again" (v. 35). This perhaps was the most remarkable accomplishment of faith, and yet there were some who perceived by faith that there is a greater accomplishment than this—a better resurrection. This "better resurrection" was to be accomplished through the resurrection of Jesus Christ. The greatest and ultimate achievement of faith is resurrection.

In all of these pictures of the accomplishments of faith, the underlying lesson is that faith does accomplish great things, both physically and spiritually. Through faith people have accomplished the impossible.

These accomplishments may come about in either one of two ways, sometimes in both. There are times when faith accomplishes its goal by causing a miracle to be performed. It was through such a miracle that the Israelites were able to cross the Red Sea and thus obtain their deliverance. It was through such a miracle that Jericho was conquered, thus giving the children of Israel entrance into the Land of Promise. It was through such a miracle that Israel was saved from the wicked hands of Ahab and Jezebel. It was through such a miracle that the three Hebrew children were protected from the heat of the fiery furnace. It was through such a miracle that Simon Peter was saved from death that he might continue to preach the gospel.

Through the ages, many great accomplishments have been made possible by the working of miracles growing out of faith. Through faith such miracles are still possible in the achieving of that which is pleasing to God.

At other times the accomplishments of faith come through renewed courage and determination which faith inspires. Faith keeps a person inexorably working at the task until it is complete. With lesser faith or no faith, the same person might give up in despair. Faith keeps us pressing toward the mark until the goal is reached. Without faith there can be no incentive or determination. Through such determined dedication, great things are accomplished. In each case the cause can be traced back to faith.

What Faith Enables Us to Endure

Faith is not always on the offense. Sometimes it is on the defense. When faith is on the defense, patient endurance is the result. Therefore, in relating the achievement of faith the writer of our epistle has shown what faith has caused believers to endure. These people of faith were tortured, subjected to cruel mockings, scourgings, and imprisonments, stoned, sawn asunder, tried, slain with the sword, and cast out. These people of faith endured such trials without whimpering or waivering. Faith gave them the patience to endure the severest kind of affliction and persecution.

Faith often finds its finest expression in graceful endurance of that which is unpleasant. It may take more faith to endure gracefully the trials of life than it does to keep working at the task assigned; however, it takes a good measure of faith to do well at either.

Through faith, sufferers are able to see the ephemeral nature of their sufferings. Through faith these know that the sufferings are not forever. Also through faith, one can see beyond the suffering to a blessed peace. Even if the suffering is unto death, faith causes us to see beyond death and to know that even if the suffering kills us there is a blessed tomorrow beyond death.

Without such faith to see the heavenly bliss beyond death, one could not endure the trials of life.

The Old Testament persons mentioned in this eleventh chapter of Hebrews were not the only ones who were able to endure trials and persecutions through faith. History is replete with other examples, such as Polycarp, the beloved bishop of Smyrna in the second century AD. After a series of persecutions, he was finally carried before the proconsul, condemned, and burned in the market place. Just before his burning, the proconsul urged him to reproach Christ with the promise that he would be released. But Polycarp replied, "Eighty and six years have I served him, and he never once wronged me; how then shall I blaspheme my King, who hath saved me?"[2]

Another good example of faith for the enduring of persecution is the case of John Huss, who in the early part of the fifteenth century was burned at the stake by papal authority as a heretic. As he was led to the stake, they placed upon his head a paper miter on which was written these words, "A ring leader of heretics." When John Huss saw it, he publicly testified with these words, "My Lord Jesus Christ, for my sake, did wear a crown of thorns; why should not I then, for His sake, again wear this light crown, be it ever so ignominious? Truly I will do it, and that willingly." Then, lifting up his eyes toward heaven, said "I do commend into Thy hands, O Lord Jesus Christ, my spirit which Thou hast redeemed." As the flames enveloped his body, he was heard to say, "I never preached any doctrine of an evil tendency; and what I taught with my lips I now seal with my blood." These words were followed with the singing of a hymn which was so loud and cheerful that he was heard through all the cracklings of the combustibles and the noise of the multitude.[3]

When one is led through the valley of the shadow of death by the death of a loved one, faith makes all the difference in the world. Some are completely overcome by the sorrow, sinking to the depth of despair and emotional breakdown. Others are able to bear up under the sorrow with peace and tranquillity. Once

I stood by the side of a devoted Christian woman who had just lost a beloved companion rather suddenly and unexpectedly. Of course, her heart was pained by this loss, but she did not fall apart. Instead she faced up to the situation with a real sense of peace within. When I made some remark about her beautiful attitude, she replied: "Without faith I just couldn't stand it." I was not surprised to hear her make a statement like that, for I had already diagnosed her situation and had concluded that faith made it possible for her to endure the trial so graciously. Faith does make a difference when one is brought face-to-face with some great trial or tribulation.

Faith is meaningful in any kind of a trial, but especially in a trial of persecution when one is subjected to the afflictions of people simply because one is a Christian. Most of us know very little about this kind of trial, but some of our forebears knew the trials quite well and the day may come when those who call themselves Christians will be subjected to the same kind of cruel treatment at the hands of people. If and when it does come, may we be found with the same kind of faith which characterized these men of old such as Jeremiah, Isaiah, Daniel, Stephen, Peter, and Paul. Faith caused Peter and John to say, after they had been mercilessly beaten by the Jewish leaders, that they rejoiced to be counted worthy to suffer for the name of Jesus. They knew, by faith, that out of that suffering would come blessing and glory to the name of the Lord Jesus. Faith reaches its highest level when one is confronted with suffering in the form of persecution. Faith is meaningful and necessary in any kind of suffering, but it is most significant when that suffering grows directly out of our devotion to Christ.

Such suffering may take any one of several different forms, as indicated in our text. It may be physical torture, vilification, loneliness, or death. In any case, it involves a testing of faith. Faith causes a person to stand up to any of these tests with a peaceful tranquillity within and a pleasant smile without. Stephen gave a demonstration of this kind of faith when he was stoned to death by the enemies of Christ. The Scripture tells us that his face shone as the face of an angel, and he prayed, "Father, lay not this sin to their charge." This conduct and attitude on the part of Stephen can be explained by one thing only—faith. By faith he could see beyond death into the face of the Lord Himself.

Whether it is in the realm of accomplishment or endurance, faith is the victory. There may be a question as to when faith changes from one realm into the other. Men and women of faith will never give up in their desire and efforts to accomplish something positive; however, there are certain times and conditions when one can do little more than express one's faith by patient endurance. There is a sad lack of faith when one thinks only in terms of endurance under any circumstance. In fact, there is not a sharp line of demarcation which can be drawn between these two realms. Usually we are involved with both realms at the same time, though there are times when one is predominant over the other. Faith is not satisfied with mere endurance alone when there is something to be accomplished on the active side.

By faith we accomplish the worthwhile; by faith we endure the unpleasant. One is as much an achievement of faith as the other, but in people of faith one is never found alone. Where one is found, the other will be found also. They are coinhabiters of the life of faith. The faith of our fathers was a double-barreled faith—it wrought wonders, and it endured trials. Let us say with Frederick W. Faber:

> Faith of our fathers! living still
>   In spite of dungeon, fire, and sword,
> O how our hearts beat high with joy
>   When e'er we hear that glorious word!
> Faith of our fathers, holy faith!
>   We will be true to thee till death.

14
The Challenge of Faith

The first three verses of the twelfth chapter of the Epistle to the Hebrews really belong to the eleventh chapter. The chapter division suggests to the reader that a new thought has been introduced, but in this case it is not so. These three verses constitute the climax of the author's great discourse on faith. It is an appeal or exhortation based upon the review of faith which he has just given, using as examples many of the outstanding people of the Old Testament. The "wherefore" ties this appeal to that which has immediately preceded. In the light of the examples of faith given in the eleventh chapter, this passionate appeal is directed to the readers of the epistle:

> Wherefore seeing we also are compassed about with so great a cloud of witnesses, let us lay aside every weight, and the sin which doth so easily beset us, and let us run with patience the race that is set before us, Looking unto Jesus the author and finisher of our faith; who for the joy that was set before him endured the cross, despising the shame, and is set down at the right hand of the throne of God. For consider him that endured such contradiction of sinners against himself, lest ye be wearied and faint in your minds (12:1-3).

Herein is the challenge of faith. In this challenge, four key words shall guide our thoughts in this exposition. The first word upon which we will focus our attention is that little four-letter word *race*. The second thought is suggested by the word *witnesses*. The third division of our discourse finds its inspiration in the verb *lay aside.* This suggests preparation. Another verb, *run,* suggests our final thought of performance.

The Race

If we are to feel the full force of this challenge, we must first envision the situation as depicted in our text. By way of analogy, the author pictured life as a great arena in which people are running in a race. This is one of the most interesting and revealing of the biblical analogies depicting life on earth. Paul used it several times in his epistles, such as in 1 Corinthians 9:24-27. Life is a race, and we are all running in it. There may be a sense in which we are competing against one another, but actually it is not so much a competing against one another as it is a competing against time and contrary winds. In the race of life, there is more than one winner.

But to win in this race of life, one must give oneself without reservation to the running. Life's trophies are not won by a leisurely trot around the arena. The strenuousness of the race is suggested by the word which the author used in our text. It is the word *agōna* from which we get our English word *agony.* It suggests the exertion of energy. The runner strains every muscle in his body to reach the goal.

It should be understood by all that life is no playground where aimless and leisurely actions are pursued without effort or purpose. Running the race of life is serious business, and it demands complete and purposeful dedication. Too many people think of life as a playground instead of a racing arena. This is not to say that life affords no pleasures, but pleasures are much sweeter and more enduring for those who take life seriously.

The Witnesses

The writer said that in this race of life we are surrounded with a "great cloud of witnesses" (12:1). Who are these witnesses, and just what is their relation to us? It is quite obvious that "witnesses" refers to the people mentioned in the eleventh chapter—the great heroes of faith, such as Abel, Enoch, Noah,

Abraham, Sara, Isaac, Jacob, Joseph, Moses, Joshua,˙ and Rahab. These and other people of faith constitute the cloud of witnesses. It would be safe to assume that it would include all Christians of all time who have died in the faith.

In what sense, then, are these people witnesses to those who are now running in the race? Some have interpreted this verse to mean that these Old Testament saints are actually sitting in the stands of the arena of life looking on as we run. Such an interpretation would make the word *witness* synonymous with the word *spectator*. A. C. Kendrick, in the *American Commentary,* gives such an interpretation:

> The author now transfers his readers to a Grecian race course, along whose sides are grouped as spectators the whole long line of distinguished confessors and champions of the faith, whom he has just enumerated. Instead of coldly appealing to the memory and the reason, he by a magic sweep of his pen brings the whole body of them around his readers, and thus brings to bear upon them not only the force of their example, but of their ideal presence . . . From their home in the clouds, from their heavenly rest, they are actually bending down to behold us.[1]

Such a picture is sentimentally significant, but it has no real scriptural basis. In fact, the word which the writer used here— *martus*—is not used in the New Testament in the sense of a spectator. The witnesses were persons who by their speech and actions had testified to the value of faith. They were people whose lives had given testimony to triumphs of faith in life and in death. Marcus Dods explained that "the idea is not that they are running in the presence of spectators and must therefore run well; but that their people's history being filled with examples of much-enduring but triumphant faith, they also must approve their lineage by showing a like persistence of faith."[2]

B. F. Westcott believed that both ideas are involved here.[3] While he insisted that the primary idea is that of witness to the validity of faith, he also believed, because of the analogy of the arena, that the writer thought of these Old Testament saints as being present in the stands in the sense that their testimonies were or should be ever present to the mind of the runner. Both Leon Morris and Philip Edcumbe Hughes agree with this interpretation.[4] Even though some such idea as this may be allowed, I could never concur in the idea that saints in heaven are now looking down upon their loved ones and friends, as people would sit in the stands and watch the runner in the race. There is nothing in the Scripture to indicate that saints in glory are conscious of what is going on here on earth. If they could know what is going on here below, their bliss in heaven would surely be mutilated. The saints in glory are ever-present witnesses to us, testifying to the validity and power of faith, but they are not spectators looking on from the stands while we run. An old song which was at one time very popular may have a sentimental attraction, but it is theologically unsound:

> Looking this way; yes, looking this way,
> Loved ones in glory are looking this way.

All people of faith, both past and present, are constant and ever-present witnesses to me in this struggle of life, but I cannot believe that they have turned their eyes away from the glories of heaven to watch the sordid scenes below.

The Preparation

We are exhorted to "lay aside every weight, and the sin which doth so easily beset us" (v. 1). This part of the exhortation speaks of the preparation for the running of the race. Two things must be laid aside if the runner is to run with endurance: weight and besetting sin. The two words as used in our text are both interesting and enlightening.

The first word is "weight." It is found only here in the New Testament, and it carries the idea of bulk of body or excessive weight. Before runners can do their best in the race, they must get rid of excessive weight. It is not that the excessive weight is bad in itself, but it does hinder and hold back. One of the first things any athlete does at the beginning of the season is to get rid of the excessive weight which has accumulated during the off season.

It is just the same in the race of life. We have a tendency to build up excessive weight, that is, we take on things which, though in themselves are not necessarily evil, hinder the best performance. Christians do many things which are not evil in themselves, but they sap the energy which could be used in the main race. B. F. Westcott explained it like this:

> The writer seems to have in his mind the manifold encumbrances of society and business which would be likely to hinder a Christian convert. The duty of the convert would be to free himself from associations and engagements which, however innocent in themselves, hindered the freedom of his action.[5]

The work of faith is often hindered by good people who allow themselves to become so preoccupied with other good but secondary activities that they are not able to give their best effort to the main task. If we would have victory in the work of faith, we must be willing to lay aside these extracurricular activities and give ourselves with utter abandon to the main task at hand.

The second thing to be laid aside in preparation for the race of life is besetting sin. The adjective which qualifies "sin" here has been variously interpreted. It could refer to that which is "easy to put off," "popularly supported," or "readily besetting." It is a compound word made up of three words or parts of words: *eu, peri,* and *statos.* Putting the last two together, the sense would be that of something standing around as an enclosure. *Eu* carries the idea of that which is well or effective. When used as a qualifying adjective for "sin," it would suggest the sin by which we are practically encircled. The presence of the article suggests the particular sin to which one is most vulnerable. The author was not thinking of sin in general, nor of sin in its gross form, for he was talking to Christians whose sins had been redeemed. But even for Christians, there are those little "pet sins" which seem to hang around to tantalize us and incapacitate us for the running of the race. Let us see to it that these little besetting sins are laid aside so that we can run the race without hindrance. These little sins are like a robe cast about the body of the runner. One must cast off this robe if one is to run with effectiveness. Even so must we cast off the robes of besetting sin if we would run the race with victory.

The Performance

Having laid aside the excessive weight and the besetting sin, we are ready to run. In the performance, two things must be remembered. First, we are to run with patience. The writer did not mean to imply by his use of *patience* that we are to run the race of life without concern or excitement. To some people, patience may mean lying down and taking whatever happens to come along without getting upset. But this is not the true meaning of the word which is used in our text. Perhaps a better translation would be "steadfastness or endurance." It carries the idea of steadfast dedication to the task until the goal is reached. To run with patience is not to run nonchalantly. There is nothing incompatible between enthusiasm and patience. To run with patience is to run with enthusiasm and dedication without wavering or falling by the wayside. One who runs with patience runs with all of his heart until he crosses the finishing line. This is the challenge of faith.

Second, we are to run with our eyes upon Jesus, "Looking unto Jesus the author and finisher of our faith" (v. 2). Herein is the real secret of success in the running of the race of life. The writer wanted his readers to know that while the saints of the Old Testament were witnesses to faith and examples of faith, they were not to be held up as objects of faith. They simply testified concerning God and His Son. We must look with faith to the Son. This, then, is the punch line. It is so easy for us to lose the race while looking at ourselves or at those who are about us. Successful runners must learn to keep their eyes on the goal, never losing sight of it. In the race of life, that goal is Jesus. We should ever strive to be where He is and to be like

Him. The word used in our text carries the idea of looking away from other things to Jesus, the God-man who became sin for us and who now lives to make intercession for us.

Jesus is both "the author and finisher of our faith." The first word suggests example. Christ is represented here, not so much as the originator of faith as the beginner, forerunner, or leader of all in the long procession of people of faith. We need to look to Him because He is the finest example of faith. The following interesting comment came from the pen of the gifted expositor Alexander Maclaren:

> Here in our text one solitary figure shines out, and all the "cloud of witnesses" fades away like morning mist.
> Christ's place is apart from theirs. They stand grouped together, the army of the faithful; He stands alone, its Captain and Commander. Their lives may be a motive for perseverance, and we may say "seeing we are compassed about with so great a cloud . . . let us run with patience." But He gives the power by which we can run, and "looking unto Jesus" is the condition on which alone we can fulfil the command.[6]

Jesus furnishes us not only with the finest example of faith but also is the "finisher" of faith. The word carries the idea of perfecting. We are to look to Jesus because He is the one who perfects faith. The result of faith in Christ is more faith. When we use what little faith we have to look up to Him, He begins to work in us and to perfect that faith which has been begun. We must see more in Jesus than a mere example. He will perfect our faith by injecting into us His sovereign power by which we accomplish the noblest victories. This He does through discipline and sorrow as well as through direct injection.

There are many important things to remember in running the race of life, but the most important of all is that we must keep our eyes on Jesus. This lesson is vividly illustrated in the game of golf which I play with enjoyment and yet with embarrassing imperfection. There are many important things to remember in the game of golf, such as right stance, smooth back swing, complete follow-through, but most important of all is the keeping of the eyes upon the ball. The other things are of no value if one does not keep one's eye on the ball. Even so, in the game of life all other good things are of no avail if we do not keep our eyes on Jesus. Helen Lemmel has expressed this truth in these beautiful poetic words:

> O soul, are you weary and troubled?
> No light in the darkness you see?
> There's light for a look at the Savior,
> And life more abundant and free!

> Thro' death into life everlasting
> He passed, and we follow him there;
> Over us sin no more hath dominion—
> For more than conq'rors we are!

> His word shall not fail you—he promised;
> Believe Him, and all will be well:
> Then go to a world that is dying,
> His perfect salvation to tell!

> Turn your eyes upon Jesus,
> Look full in his wonderful face,
> And the things of earth will grow strangely dim
> In the light of his glory and grace.[7]

15

The Victory of Faith

In challenging readers to greater faith, the author of the Epistle to the Hebrews pointed to Jesus "who for the joy that was set before him endured the cross, despising the shame, and is set down at the right hand of the throne of God" (12:2). This is the climactic conclusion to this masterful discourse on the subject of faith. It reveals the victory of faith—a transcendent and inextricable joy—a joy which is best exemplified in Jesus as He faced the cross.

Usually in our thinking, we associate the cross with pain and suffering. Here it is associated with joy, thus giving to us another interesting and significant paradox. This is not to say that the cross, of itself and by itself, was a joy or pleasure to experience, but it does mean that there was a joy associated with this experience of the cross. What was this joy, and where was it to be found?

Without trying to be exhaustive, let me point out four joys which Jesus must have associated with the cross experience. All of these were products of faith.

The Joy of a Finished Task

In the experience of the cross, Jesus completed a task which had been assigned to Him—the task of making an atonement for sin. This is not to say that all of Jesus' work was finished on the cross. His work of intercession continues as long as people live upon this earth. But His work of atonement was finished on the cross. As the writer of this epistle said frequently, Jesus made one once-for-all, all-sufficient sacrifice for sin on Calvary. The sacrifices of the Old Testament had to be repeated over and over, but the one sacrifice of Jesus on the cross was sufficient for all time. Therefore, we can say that the work of atonement was finished on the cross. It needs no continuation or repetition. For this reason, Jesus could say as He hung on the cross, "It is finished" (John 19:30).

This consciousness of having finished a task assigned must have given to Jesus a sense of real joy and satisfaction. This was doubtlessly a part of the joy which He saw before Him as He faced the crucial and agonizing experiences of the cross. There is always a feeling of joy when one comes to the finishing mark of a task, and the more difficult and arduous the task the greater is the joy. There is no way to measure the joy that must have flooded the soul of Jesus when He looked back over His earthly life from His crucial position on the cross to say: "It is finished."

The same kind of joy will be ours, even though in smaller measure, if, at the end of life's journey, we can look back over a life which has been spent in the service of the Lord. Few words bring more regret and remorse than the word *unfinished*. On the other hand, few words bring more joy and satisfaction than the word *finished*. The words of an old hymn express this joy for us:

> The sands have been washed in the footprints
> Of the Stranger on Galilee's shore—
> And the voice that subdued the rough billows
> Will be heard in Judea no more.
> But the path of that lone Galilean
> With joy I will follow today;
> And the toils of the road will seem nothing,
> When I get to the end of the way.

> When the last feeble steps have been taken,
> And the gates of that city appear,
> And the beautiful songs of the angels
> Float out on my listening ear;
> When all that now seems so mysterious

Will be bright and as clear as the day;
Then the toils of the road will seem nothing,
When I get to the end of the way.

The Joy of a Heavenly Reunion

Beyond the cross was reunion with the Father. The cross, therefore, became a joy to Jesus because through it He was able to return to the Father and sit down on the Father's right hand. There was a certain intimate fellowship which Jesus maintained throughout His earthly life with the Father, but it was nothing like the fellowship which He enjoyed with the Father before He descended to this world of sin and woe. And there was a moment when this fellowship was broken off completely. At that moment when Jesus became sin for us by taking our place on the cross, the Father turned His back on the Son, insomuch that the Son cried out, "My God, my God, why hast thou forsaken me?" (Matt. 27:46). God could not countenance sin, and He had to break off this intimate relationship when the Son became sin for us. But this fellowship was not broken off forever. Beyond the cross, it was restored.

This was the joy which Jesus experienced in the cross. Foreseeing this reunion as He faced the cross, He could pray to the Father in this manner: "I have glorified thee on the earth: I have finished the work which thou gavest me to do. And now, O Father, glorify thou me with thine own self with the glory which I had with thee before the world was" (John 17:4-5). Jesus looked beyond the cross to see a restoration of fellowship with the Father like that which He had with the Father before He came into this world, and He rejoiced. Is there a greater joy than the joy of returning home after one has been away for a long period? The cross was the last lap on the Savior's return to His heavenly home. No matter how weary one may be with the hardships and trials of the way, one experiences a deep inner joy when one catches sight of home and reunion with loved ones. Jesus looked from the cross to see the sight of His heavenly home and the reunion with His father and breathed a sigh of relief and joy.

A similar joy is ours when we are led through loneliness and tribulation in the service of the Lord, if we can look by faith beyond the trials into the heavenly home where there is reunion with redeemed loved ones. The sight of this heavenly home is enough to give joy in the darkest night.

The Joy of a Heavenly Exaltation

Christ not only saw through the cross a restored fellowship with the Father but also He saw a heavenly exaltation. The path to the cross had led through humiliation and ignominy; but Jesus knew that beyond the cross was glory. Having endured the cross, He sat down (perfect tense signifying permanent position) on the right hand of the throne of God. This, to be sure, involved restored fellowship with God, but it also involved a position of honor and exaltation. The enduring of the cross became an experience of joy in the light of the glory which He could see beyond it.

The trials of this life take on a brighter hue when by faith we look beyond the trial into the glory which shall be ours in the heavenly surroundings. It is this hope which gives to the Christian determination and optimism in the face of bitter trials. The apostle Paul said, "For I reckon that the sufferings of this present time are not worthy to be compared with the glory which shall be revealed in us" (Rom. 8:18). He also said, "For our light affliction, which is but for a moment, worketh for us a far more exceeding and eternal weight of glory" (2 Cor. 4:17). Any trial is more bearable when we can see through it into a glorious state of bliss. Trials and tribulations become occasions of joy when we can sing with William Hunter:

> My heavenly home is bright and fair,
> Nor pain nor death can enter there;
> Its glittering towers the sun outshine,
> That heavenly mansion shall be mine.

My Father's house is built on high,
  Far, far above the starry sky;
When from this earthly prison free,
  That heavenly mansion mine shall be.

Let others seek a home below,
  Which flames devour, or waves o'er flow;
Be mine a happier lot to own
  A heavenly mansion near the throne.

I'm going home, I'm going home,
  I'm going home to die no more,
To die no more, to die no more;
  I'm going home to die no more.

The Joy of an Accomplished Redemption

The greatest joy which Jesus found in the cross was the joy of a accomplished redemption for fallen humanity. While He must have found a measure of joy in the thought of a heavenly exaltation following the cross experience, it was by no means a selfish joy. He rejoiced in the thought of exaltation and glory because He knew that through that experience on the cross others would be able to share that exaltation with Him. Had it been only an exaltation for Himself alone, it would have had little attraction or meaning to Him. He wanted this glory to share it with the redeemed family.

Jesus looked into the cross experience and through it to see that out of it would come glory, not only for Himself but also for a vast army of fallen humanity. The joy was more than the joy of a finished task; it was more than the joy of a heavenly exaltation for Himself. When He by faith anticipated the multitudes of people who would be redeemed by that cross experience and brought into the glory of a heavenly and eternal bliss, He surely must have thought that it was worth it all. Jesus attached great importance to the human soul. He saw every person was an eternal soul; He also saw every person as a condemned soul because of sin. To think that many people would be redeemed through His sacrifice for sin on the cross was a thought that must have thrilled Him more than any other.

When one loves another, a sacrifice, however great, in order to save that one from a terrible catastrophe is not too great. It is welcomed as an opportunity. This is something of the joy which Jesus found in the cross. The experience itself was not pleasant, but He found pleasure in knowing what it would do for people whom He loved. It would make possible their redemption and their ultimate glorification with Him. The thought of his own glorification would have meant little to Him had it not been mingled with the thought of the glorification of all those who would be redeemed by His sacrifice. Marcus Dods is right in saying, "This joy was the sitting in the place of achieved victory and power, not a selfish joy, but the consciousness of salvation wrought for men, of power won which He could use in their interests."[1]

All of these joys, and more, added together simply meant that the benefits growing out of the cross far outweighed the suffering which was involved in it. Therefore, Jesus endured it with determination and optimism. Two lessons we all should learn from this experience. In the first place, we should learn that true joy does not come by eliminating or avoiding pain and trial. In fact, true joy sometimes comes through pain and trial, not just any pain or trial but through those trials which produce the greater benefits. There is no virtue in suffering as such, but suffering which is redemptive or beneficial in some way to others becomes the source and inspiration for the most meaningful joys of life. True joy, then, is to be found not in searching out the easiest and most comfortable way but in the investment of life in the service of others. Such an investment as that requires sacrifice and inconvenience.

In the second place, we should learn that the greatest joy is to be found not in the present circumstance or condition but in the anticipation of that which is yet future. The joy which Jesus found in the cross was not in that which existed at the moment but in that which He could see by faith in the future as growing out of that which was present. Where there is no faith, there is no future; where there is no future, there is no joy. Therefore, joy is wrapped up in faith, and herein is the victory of faith. Alexander Maclaren summed up this thought in these significant words:

> Every man's life is ennobled in the measure in which he lives for a future. Even if it be a poor and near future, in so far as it is future, such a life is better than a life that is lived for the present. . . . To be absorbed in the present moment is to be degraded to the level of the beasts.[2]

Thus have we come to a fitting climax of this whole subject of faith which began with the first verse of the eleventh chapter of Hebrews. We have seen faith in its various expressions as exemplified in the saints of the Old Testament. On the basis of these examples, a challenge was issued to all of us in order that we might run with patience the race of life. Then the climax of this challenge is to be found in the words of our text: "Looking unto Jesus the author and finisher of our faith; who for the joy that was set before him endured the cross, despising the shame, and is set down at the right hand of the throne of God" (12:2).

Epilogue

In this exposition of the eleventh chapter of Hebrews, we have seen various facets of faith, looking at it from many different points of view. Though it has been alluded to several times, perhaps an addendum should be added in clarification of the significance of faith in the area of salvation.

Throughout the New Testament, the word *faith* is used in connection with the idea of salvation. Faith and belief are translations of the same Greek word, *pistis* or *pisteuō*. This word, either in its noun or verb form, appears more than five hundred times in the New Testament. Many of these references are related to the doctrine of salvation. Therefore, faith holds a prominent and necessary place in salvation; however, there is considerable misunderstanding among people generally as to the proper significance of faith in salvation. Perhaps one of the clearest statements in the Bible setting forth the relation of faith to salvation is found in Ephesians 2:8-9: "For by grace are ye saved through faith; and that not of yourselves: it is the gift of God: Not of works, lest any man should boast."

The Meaning of Faith

We must first understand the meaning of the word *faith*. The word is used in at least three senses in the New Testament. These can be detected by a careful examination of the context.

Sometimes the word refers to a body of truth or a doctrine, such as when Jude urged his readers to "earnestly contend for the faith which was once delivered unto the saints" (v. 3).

Faith is also used to refer to the acceptance of a fact or doctrine as being true. This is what we sometimes call intellectual belief or faith. This is the predominant idea of faith as expressed in the Epistle of James, concerning which James declared that this kind of faith is not sufficient. He reminded his readers that even the devils believe in this sense. They believe that there is one God and tremble at the thought of Him (Jas. 2:19). This is not saving faith.

The third sense in which *faith* is used means a personal trust or commitment. This is the prevalent meaning of the word in the Epistles of Paul. This is what Paul meant when he said, "Therefore we conclude that a man is justified by faith without the deeds of the law" (Rom. 3:28). Faith in the sense of personal trust is essential to salvation, and anything less than this is totally invalid so far as salvation is concerned.

The Objectivity of Faith

While faith is essential to salvation, it is important that we understand the object of that faith. It is not just faith in anything or anybody. It must be a faith objectified in Jesus Christ. Actually, faith does not save; Jesus Christ saves. Faith is simply the instrument through which Jesus saves. Of course, He will not save except through faith, but it is not "our" faith that saves us. Some people seem to have faith in their faith, and this is the same as no faith at all. Faith is absolutely valueless unless it is objectified in Jesus. But Christ has chosen to bestow His salvation by grace through our faith, and never apart from it.

The Potential of Faith

Faith is not only the means by which Christ bestows His salvation upon us but also the means through which He bestows upon us blessings untold in our Christian lives. Faith continues to grow the more we use it. Faith is like the muscle in the arm—the more it is challenged and used, the stronger it gets. The less it is used, the weaker it becomes. Therefore, we are exhorted throughout the Scriptures to exercise our faith not only to accomplish great things in the service of the Lord but also to strengthen our own faith for greater blessings in the future. With the disciples of old, let us pray: "Lord, Increase our faith" (Luke 17:5), for even our faith comes from God (Eph. 2:8).

Notes

CHAPTER 1

1. Arthur W. Pink, *An Exposition of Hebrews* (Grand Rapids, Mich.: Baker Book House, 1954), p. 649.

2. A. C. Kendrick, *American Commentary* (Philadelphia: American Baptist Publishing Society), 6, p. 145.

3. Thomas Arnold, *Christianity Today,* 1 Sept. 1958, p. 39.

4. Leon Morris, "Hebrews," *The Expositor's Bible Commentary,* Frank E. Gaebelein, ed. (Grand Rapids, Mich.: Zondervan, 1981), 12, p. 113.

5. John Owen, *Exercitations on the Epistle to the Hebrews* (Edinburgh, 1855), p. 115.

6. Marcus Dods, "The Epistle to the Hebrews," *Expositor's Greek Testament,* W. Robertson Nicoll, ed. (Grand Rapids, Mich.: Wm. B. Eerdmans, n.d.), 4, p. 352.

7. Owen, p. 116.

8. G. Campbell Morgan, *The Westminster Pulpit* (New York: Fleming H. Revell, 1954), 4, p. 297.

CHAPTER 2

1. W. E. Denham, "Making a World," *Southwestern Journal of Theology,* 5, no. 4, p. 3.

2. Harold B. Kuhn, "Creation," *Christianity Today,* 8 May 1961, p. 22.

3. W. B. Tolar, "Religious Faith in a Scientific Age or The Creation: Chance or Choice?" (Ft. Worth: Southwestern Baptist Theological Seminary, 1978: unpublished paper), p. 3.

4. Ibid., p. 8.

CHAPTER 3
1. Marcus Dods, "The Epistle to the Hebrews." *Expositor's Greek Testament* W. Robertson Nicoll, ed. (Grand Rapids, Mich.: Wm. B. Eerdmans, n.d.), 4, p. 353.
2. *A Commentary on the Epistle to the Hebrews* (Grand Rapids, Mich.: Wm. B. Eerdmans, 1977), p. 455.
3. B. F. Westcott, *The Epistle to the Hebrews* (New York: Macmillan and Co., 1889), p. 354.

CHAPTER 4
1. Marcus Dods, "The Epistle to the Hebrews," *Expositor's Greek Testament,* W. Robertson Nicoll, ed. (Grand Rapids, Mich.: Wm. B. Eedrmans, n.d.), 4, p. 354.
2. G. Campbell Morgan, *The Westminster Pulpit* (New York: Fleming H. Revell, 1955), 10, p. 143.
3. W. A. Criswell, *These Issues We Must Face* (Grand Rapids, Mich.: Zondervan, 1953), p. 16.
4. Ibid., p. 12.
5. B. F. Westcott, *The Epistle to the Hebrews* (New York: Macmillan and Co., 1889), p. 356.
6. Philip E. Hughes, *A Commentary on the Epistle to the Hebrews* (Grand Rapids, Mich.: Wm. B. Eerdmans, 1977), p. 458.
7. I. B. Sergei, "My God and I," © Copyright 1935. Renewal by Austris Whithol. Assigned to Singspiration, Division of the Zondervan Corporation. All rights reserved. Used by permission.

CHAPTER 5
1. W. A. Criswell, *The Gospel According to Moses* (Nashville: Broadman Press, 1950), p. 13.
2. Ibid., p. 15.
3. J. Weiss cited by Marcus Dods, "The Epistle to the Hebrews," *Expositor's Greek Testament,* W. Robertson Nicoll, ed. (Grand Rapids, Mich.: Wm. B. Eerdmans, n.d.), 4, p. 355.
4. Dods, ibid.
5. J. H. Thayer, *Greek-English Lexicon of the New Testament* (New York: American Book Co., 1889), p. 332.
6. B. F. Westcott, *The Epistle to the Hebrews* (New York: Macmillan and Co., 1889), p. 357.

CHAPTER 6

1. Richard Watson, *Sermons and Sketches of Sermons*(New York: G. Lane and C. B. Tippett, 1848), 2, p. 124.

2. B. F. Westcott, *The Epistle to the Hebrews*(New York: Macmillan and Co., 1889), p. 357.

CHAPTER 7

1. G. Campbell Morgan, "Christian Citizenship: No Abiding City," *The Westminster Pulpit*(New York: Fleming H. Revell, 1955), 5, p. 140.

2. Philip E. Hughes, *A Commentary on the Epistle to the Hebrews* (Grand Rapids, Mich.: Wm. B. Eerdmans, 1977), p. 476.

3. Leon Morris, *The Expositor's Bible Commentary*, Frank E. Gaebelein, ed. (Grand Rapids, Mich.: Zondervan, 1981), 12, p. 120.

CHAPTER 8

1. Marcus Dods, "The Book of Genesis," *The Expositor's Bible*, W. Robertson Nicoll, ed. (New York: Armstrong and Son, 1907), 1, p. 198.

2. C. F. Keil and F. Delitzsch, *Biblical Commentary on the Old Testament, Pentateuch* (Grand Rapids, Mich.: Wm. B. Eerdmans, 1949), 1, p. 248.

3. Dods, pp. 199-200.

4. B. F. Westcott, *The Epistle to the Hebrews*(New York: Macmillan and Co., 1889), p. 365.

5. Ibid., p. 367.

CHAPTER 9

1. Leon Morris, "Hebrews," *The Expositor's Bible Commentary*, Frank E. Gaebelein, ed. (Grand Rapids, Mich.: Zondervan, 1981), 12, p. 123.

2. A. J. Gordon, *The First Thing in the World*(New York: Fleming H. Revell, 1891), p. 12.

3. Russell H. Conwell, *Life of Charles Haddon Spurgeon*(Edgewood Pub. Co., 1892), p. 406 *ff.*

CHAPTER 10

1. B. F. Westcott, *The Epistle to the Hebrews*(New York: Macmillan and Co., 1889), p. 371.

2. Leon McBeth, *Men Who Made Missions*(Nashville, Tenn.: Broadman Press, 1968), pp. 70 *ff.*

3. W. M. Taylor, *Contrary Winds and Other Sermons* (New York: Richard R. Smith, 1930), p. 121.

4. Ibid., pp. 123 *ff.*

CHAPTER 11

1. See Alfred Weber, *History of Philosophy* (New York: Charles Scribner's Sons, 1901), pp. 323-434.

2. See Carl F. H. Henry, *God, Revelation and Authority* (Waco, Tex.: Word Books, 1976), pp. 96-213.

3. Harry Emerson Fosdick, *The Modern Use of the Bible* (New York: Macmillan and Co., 1924), p. 157.

4. Fred Fisher, *The Purpose of God and the Christian Life* (Philadelphia: Westminster Press, 1962), p. 30.

5. C. A. Beckworth, "Miracles," *The New Schaff-Herzog Encyclopedia of Religious Knowledge* (Grand Rapids, Mich.: Baker Book House, 1951), 7, pp. 385-388.

6. Ibid., p. 31.

7. John W. Peterson, "It Took a Miracle," © Copyright 1948 by John W. Peterson Music Co. All Rights Reserved. Used by Permission.

CHAPTER 12

1. B. F. Westcott, *The Epistle to the Hebrews* (New York: Macmillan, 1889), p. 377.

2. Clarence MacCartney, *Great Women of the Bible* (New York: Abingdon-Cokesbury, 1942), p. 44.

3. Ibid., p. 50.

CHAPTER 13

1. B. F. Westcott, *The Epistle to the Hebrews* (New York: Macmillan, 1889), p. 376.

2. William Byron Forbush, ed., *Fox's Book of Martyrs* (Philadelphia: The John C. Winston Co., 1926), p. 4.

3. Ibid., p. 143.

CHAPTER 14

1. A. C. Kendrick, *The American Commentary* (Philadelphia: American Baptist Publishing Society, n.d.), p. 165.

2. Marcus Dods, "The Epistle to the Hebrews," *Expositor's Greek*

Testament, W. Robertson Nicoll, ed. (Grand Rapids: Wm. B. Eerdmans, n. d.), 4, p. 365.

3. B. F. Westcott, *The Epistle to the Hebrews*(New York: Macmillan, 1889), p. 391.

4. Leon Morris, "Hebrews," *The Expositor's Bible,* Frank E. Gaebelein, ed. (Grand Rapids, Mich.: Zondervan, 1981), 12, p. 133. See also Westcott, p. 519.

5. Westcott, p. 395.

6. Alexander Maclaren, *Christ in the Heart*(New York: Macmillan, 1887), p. 77.

7. Helen Lemmel, "Turn Your Eyes upon Jesus," © Copyright 1922. Renewal by H. H. Lemmel. Assigned to Singspiration, Inc. All rights reserved. Used by permission.

CHAPTER 15

1. Marcus Dods, "The Epistle to the Hebrews," *Expositor's Greek Testament,* W. Robertson Nicoll, ed. (Grand Rapids, Mich.: Wm. B. Eerdman, n. d.), 4, p. 366.

2. Alexander Maclaren, *Christ in the Heart*(New York: Macmillan, 1887), p. 95.